Mario Bellini

Mario Bellini Architecture 1984-1995

Edited by
Ermanno Ranzani

Introduction by
Kurt Forster

Birkhäuser
Basel · Berlin · Boston

720.8
B444b

Editorial cooperation
for the English edition
David Kerr

Design
Marcello Francone

Cover Design
Bruckmann und Partner, Basel

Layout
Eliana Gelati

Electronic paging
Claudio Nasso

Library of Congress
Cataloging-in-Publication Data
A CIP catalogue record
for this book is available from
the Library of Congress,
Washington, D.C., USA

Deutsche Bibliothek
Cataloging-in-Publication Data
Bellini, Mario:
Mario Bellini: architecture
1984-1995 / ed. by Ermanno
Ranzani. Introduction by Kurt
Forster. - Basel; Boston; Berlin:
Birkhäuser, 1996
ISBN 3-7643-5375-9 (Basel...)
ISBN 0-8176-5375-9 (Boston)

Printed on acid-free paper
produced from chlorine-free
pulp.

The material for this volume was
collected by Elena Bellini for the
exhibition "Urban Islands.
Architectural Works of Mario
Bellini 1985-1995" at the Royal
Institute of British Architects –
Architecture Centre, London,
30th January – 30th March 1996.

We should like to thank all the
collaborators in the Studio Mario
Bellini Associati and especially
Olivia De Luca.

© 1996 Skira editore, Milano, Italy
© 1996 for the English hard-
bound edition Birkhäuser – Verlag
für Architektur, P.O. Box 133,
CH-4010 Basel, Switzerland

Printed in Italy

ISBN 3-7643-5375-9
ISBN 0-8176-5375-9

9 8 7 6 5 4 3 2 1

Contents

Kurt W. Forster

Many an Urban Island:
Sites of Mario Bellini's Invention

Il grattacielo era d'argento,
supremo e felice in quella sera
bellissima e pura, mentre il vento
stirava sottili filamenti di nubi,
qua e là, sullo sfondo di un
azzurro assolutamente incredibile.
Era infatti l'ora che le città
vengono prese dall'ispirazione e chi
non è cieco ne resta travolto.[1]

"The skyscraper seemed to be of
silver, supreme and serene in the
light of this pristine and pure
evening, while the wind brushed
faint strands of clouds here and
there across a sky of absolutely
incredible azure. This was indeed
the hour when the cities are
ravished by inspiration, and
whoever is not blind will be
overwhelmed."

Mario Bellini is Milanese, a circumstance that endowed him not only with urbanity, but also habituated him to the reserve and secrecy of that city's life. Behind its elegant facades and noisy boulevards, and amid the silently decaying remnants of earlier times lie the discreet courtyards and apartments that serve Milan's peculiar culture of privacy. Such is the quasi-English face of Milan. The other face, that of Italy's preeminent city of industry and commerce, has its origins in ancient Mediolanum and the once powerful duchy of the Visconti and the Sforza which in later centuries became the administrative capital of Lombardy.

Since mediaeval times, the city has prided itself on the perfection of its nearly circular plan and the architectural power of its institutions.[2] From the Castello to the vast structure of the hospital that Filarete, inventor of the imaginary city of Sforzinda, projected for his patron in the 1460s, to the Napoleonic Forum and the Galleria Vittorio Emanuele[3] in the nineteenth century, Milan has long given rise to vast urban schemes and interventions. The tension between the magnitude of its huge frame – extending, as nowhere else in Italy, to the skyline – and the often second-hand nature of the buildings themselves has never been relieved, and may well be insoluble except in the Futurist phantoms of a Sant'Elia, or the pictorial transpositions of a Sironi.[4] If thus the urban frame and the architectural physiognomy of its contents have rarely, if ever, approached a congruence to one another, their contradictory relationship has had the effect of fracturing the coherence of every intervention while allowing the horizon to recede to ever farther reaches of the city. Hence Milan never becomes the *città analoga* Aldo Rossi imagined, but instead expands its limits like a creature forever at odds with itself. To the extent that Milan remains true to its history by re-enacting this dilemma at the core of its identity, it also lives the destiny of the modern city *tout court.*

One need not appeal to milieu theories to understand Bellini's varied activities as a constant interplay between these cultural polarities of his native city: to the demands of public life he brings his flawless sense of elegance, a keenly private trait, while he approaches with supreme confidence tasks of enormous scale, acting in worldly manner, as a professional who is conscious of the compass of his craft yet eager to nudge the limits of its power beyond conventionality.

From the pen in his hand to the furniture in his office, Bellini's reputation as an acclaimed designer has been secured by his attention to a multiplicity of forms, Today, however, the plans, models, and photographs on his drafting tables and walls mark the advent of his reputation as one of the 'young' architects of Italy – 'young' in the sense that he has been practicing as an architect for barely a decade, though his fame as a designer harks back to the 1960s.[5]

It may seem at first odd to contemplate the prospect of so accomplished a practitioner of design (the first, after Charles and Ray Eames, to be accorded a one-man show during his lifetime at the Museum of Modern Art in New York) shifting his attention to architecture. And further, the act of projecting himself into the realm of vast urban complexes rather than small precious buildings stretches the imagination. On the other hand, Italian designers usually do train as architects, and, like students of architecture everywhere, go on to pursue quite different professional careers. A few – Sottsass and Mendini among them – have taken up architecture after making a success of design; others – like Rossi – achieve as much acclaim for their product designs as they do with their buildings. What makes Bellini a special case is his virtually unmatched accomplishment as a designer, and his supreme ambition as an architect. He is disarmingly candid about what he considers the bogus mystique of design, contrived, he argues, as a means to prop up a field that cannot claim rationality (technology) or imagination (fashion) as its proper ground but must forever vacillate between the two. Bellini's adding machines, typewriters, and laptop computers for Olivetti belong to the icons of a national industry that pioneered the very idea of modern product design, while his chairs, lamps, and furniture are even more widely marketed abroad. His idea of design reveals a deeply cultural grounding that sets it apart from the fashionable hankering after effects, which has become so prevalent in the industry. He speaks of ancient Egyptian furniture as being more influential on his own designs that either ergonomics or the stylized appearance of today's objects.

Bellini's entry into architecture takes up a line of thought that emanates from his formal training, spans the years of his editorship of *Domus* (1986-91), and comes to be applied first to the traditional assignment of designing a showroom. What was rather unforeseen about the project was its location and spatial concept: the commission came from a Japanese firm, and Bellini gave it a treatment redolent of urban qualities rather than the stock-in-trade interior design. If Bellini thus inaugurated a new chapter in his career with an interior based on free-standing walls that chamber off room after room from miniature street-like corridors, his next assignment in 1984, a complex of offices and manufacturing buildings at the extreme periphery of Milan, engaged him in precisely the kind of urban intervention that has long characterized the city's expansion.

Ten years ago these buildings rose in an area of Via Kuliscioff where the city dissolved into the pastures beyond its limits. Today, they represent the only coherent complex amidst a

motley group of speculative buildings that look – and in fact are – frantically for sale. Bellini's strategy for a densely urban complex on the green pastures already displays the architectural concepts he will bring to bear on subsequent tasks. The buildings are ranged symmetrically along both sides of the road, comprising distinct units (high and low; composite or unitary) that are shifted against one another so as to position centered units face to face with intermediate ones. These fragments of a grand Milanese scheme – ample in size and tightly organized by its profile and the texture of its precast facade panels – implant at the (former) periphery the familiar urban order of the city center.

Other aspects of these office buildings are equally characteristic of Bellini's architecture and could be traced individually, as well as across their gradual transformations, throughout the evolution of his work: just as his alignment of volumes tends to imply a spinal column along which internal spaces line up with and differentiate themselves from one another, so their linear extensions, similar to streets, either converge to form plazas, or deflect from their straight paths in response to topographical or programmatic conditions. A lively play among competing forces is set in motion, but rarely is the fundamental order of these units or their conjunctions broken. The buildings on Via Kuliscioff contain *in nuce* the building blocks from which Bellini assembled his various projects throughout the 1980s. Linear continuity may prevail, but it never lacks graduated progression; individual units may assume a certain autonomy, confirmed by cylindrical stairs or patterns of fenestration, but their judicious repetition ties them into a larger frame. The very facades of these office buildings carry the code of the whole idea, for they are cast in vertical units, their raised profiles smoothly finished and their sunken panels hammered to expose the marble chips embedded in their cement aggregate.[6] Every panel represents, rather than simply reproducing, the entire system of these facades, which may claim to be as industrial as the purposes they serve.

There is yet another feature in this first project of Bellini's that will make its reappearance in later ones: in true Italian fashion, entrances always hold pride of place and receive distinctive treatment, they are brightened by the best materials and most elegant details, and they can strive to reach monumental proportions, even in the sense of 'triumphal' gateways. At Via Kuliscioff and again at the headquarters of the power plant in Cassano d'Adda, the portal assumes bridge-like dimensions, acquires lighthouse towers, and acts as true generator of the plan. In fact, one is inclined to consider an enormous structure such as the exhibition hall for the Fiera di Milano (planned in 1987 and now under construction) as a thematic enlargement of this portal typology. Spanning three full city blocks, extending over half a mile, and crossed by two avenues, the Fiera building will become Milan's largest

postwar structure, and will constitute – metaphorically as well as commercially – a massive gateway to the city. In terms of its component parts, this latecomer to urban megastructures elicits from the bridge, the portal towers, and the open pediment the hallmarks of its presence.[7] By contrast to giant buildings elsewhere, the Fiera complex will be no stranger to its city, belonging as it does to a distinct Milanese tradition of grand urban islands.

An *architectural island*, a circumscribed townscape of highly differentiated members and diverse internal cavities, represents perhaps the ideal of Bellini's work. This may explain why he is especially successful with exhibition and vacation complexes, with projects equally removed from urban congestion and suburban sprawl, yet capable of holding their own in either condition. In a number of editorials for *Domus*,[8] Bellini has attempted to define the problems that beset any architect who chooses to work within the context of the metropolis: in the wake of industrialization, the city ceases to be the preeminent site of architecture, breaking apart, instead, into conserves of the past and repositories of replacement parts. This dilemma springs from the root condition of the modern city and manifests itself differently in Tokyo, Los Angeles, New York, or Milan, but it is present in all of them and (de)pressing to the architect who would inscribe his work into their fabric.

Bellini's Tokyo Design Center (1988-92) makes the point: across from a railroad station, framing another building of the most ubiquitous commercial kind, and shielding a steep hillside with its crowning temple precinct from a divided thoroughfare, Bellini's insert into the dense urban labyrinth works like a set of theatrical masks. Toward the avenue he strengthens the prospect of two forbidding towers (wearing pyramidal caps), toward the hill that forms a natural backdrop, he opens up the building and echoes the character of the wooded slope with stepped terraces, while a diagonal corridor ascends steeply – protected by a continuous, horizontal ceiling – toward the temple.

The Tokyo Design Center possesses the facetted nature required of the *ricambio architettonico*, the interchangeability that characterizes any metropolitan replacement object, as Bellini has defined it. In its composite nature, the Center is capable of reacting to the chance encounters of its urban topography, but not without establishing a new rapport – whether diffident or intimate – with each neighbouring building. The facades conjugate the modular grids of adjacent structures, the terraces on the rear side counter the contour of a hill with their pyramidal setbacks, and the cut across the site makes for a barely visible, internal, yet nonetheless *public* passageway. If such an urban place exhibits a virtually 'fortified' character – closed and 'shuttered' with rotated cement slabs toward the street – and if the rear elevation with its massive piers and urns, remotely recalls the hybrid ornaments of a Ca' Brütta in

Milan,[9] their internal order carries the idea of a self-contained island from the level of secrecy to that of surprise.

In keeping with his notion of the metropolis as the site of exchangeable fragments and interacting events, Bellini has cultivated a capacity to act upon compromised situations. The Yokohama Business Center (1987-91), a product of the sort of speculative development that typically renders its buildings forlorn giants, offers an object lesson on Bellini's notion of *urban islands*. He remedies an apparently hopeless situation by sinking a circular pool eccentrically between the high-rise buildings, and shielding it within a mausoleum-like mound. Then he secures its seclusion as a *teatro marittimo* at the foot of an amphitheatrical ramp. The evocative power of the site draws on the imagery of the *pittura metafisica*, and thereby reminds the visitor of the peculiar state to which the modern metropolis has relegated all historic objects, the state of allegorical ruins – whether or not they have a basis in archaeology. Just as the cylinder of the Mausoleum of Augustus in Rome could, for a time, shelter a theatre, before being exposed as the empty shell it has remained ever since, the urban island for the Yokohama Business Center (ex)poses its fictional origins as a question for our own time.

However distant from the metropolis, on hilltops or at lakesides, Bellini ponders the nature of his sites and tries to locate them within a topography of his invention. The Congress Center at Cernobbio, nestled in the park of the Villa Erba on Lake Como, or the resort *Risonare* in Kobuchizawa (Japan), crowning two wooded ridges from which distant views of the Yatsugatake and, on rare days, of Mount Fuji, can be glimpsed, are just such *urban islands*. These sites are capable of holding sharply contrasting components in balance, opposing at Kobuchizawa a sort of gently curving village street with a tightly framed avenue, terminating in an amphitheatrical indoor-outdoor pool. At the Villa Erbe, the Congress Center adopts the gently sloping profile of greenhouses for its extremities, and gathers its three wings at a suspended rotunda, like spokes to the axle of a wheel, reacting to the surrounding landscape by affinity of shape or material. Bellini's generous disposition to the surroundings in fact comes across in a minor but telling detail: Where the eastern wing meets a copse of centennial sycamore trees, it lowers its roofline and simultaneously swells outward its glass curtain, as if the building were momentarily capable of assuming the flexible behaviour of an organic creature.

These architectural strategies possess sufficient flexibility and resilience to organize highly diverse ensembles in town and country. At an elementary school north of Milan (Giussano) that is now nearing completion, the classrooms form an undulating wing snaking across the triangular lot, while the urban street corner draws administrative and public quarters into a tight wedge and links them to the rear by the steeply curving roofline of a corridor that suggests the carcass of a prehistoric creature. These occasional figural elements are primarily employed to connect or conclude an architectural promenade, or tie an array of paths together, hence their narrative connection tends to confirm a functional one.

Bellini's architecture is always tied to the invention of sites: his buildings, even when free-standing, hold within themselves a multiplicity of parts and a potential plurality of references. They create islands which stand for, and intensify, the urban complexities of life. As hovering figments of the constantly interrupted and forever concatenated conditions of life, they can strike root anywhere, and thus preserve a profound desire for independence.

[1] Dino Buzzati, *La boutique del mistero*, Milan, 1968, from the short story "*Ragazza che precipita*", cited after the edition Oscar Classici moderni, Mondadori, Milan, 1993, p. 225. Buzzati, a Milanese writer belonging to the generation of Bellini's parents, established a relationship between his journalism and his surreal writings that bears comparison, *mutatis mutandis*, with the rapport between design and architecture in Bellini's work.

[2] Bonvesin de la Riva's Chronicle of the City of Milan (*De magnalibus Mediolani*, 1288) makes a point frequently taken up in subsequent representations of the city and of great importance to Filarete's idealized invention of Sforzinda.

[3] Irony would have it that the Galleria Vittorio Emanuele was substantially financed by English capital; see especially Johann Friedrich Geist, *Arcades, the History of a Building Type*, Cambridge, MA, 1983, pp. 371-401.

[4] For the evocative series of paintings, usually entitled *paesaggi urbani*, dating from the 1920s, see esp. the catalogue of the exhibition *Mario Sironi. Il mito dell'architettura*, Milan, 1990.

[5] It is widely recognized that the history of Italian art and architecture comprises a startling number of artists who turned architect, as well as architects who were active in other arts, rather than submitting to the rather rigid professional specialization that has come to be the norm.

[6] It is tempting to think in this connection of the startling treatment, characterized by regular panelling and crisp ridges, on the facade of Piero Portaluppi's Palazzo of 1926 on Corso Venezia, near Bellini's former studio, where the motif of the portal has likewise reached monumental proportions, cf. *A+U*, December extra edition (1991), 84ff.

[7] Compare the excellent article by Franco Purini, "Fiera di Milano. Sul progetto Bellini", in *Domus*, no. 728, June 1991.

[8] *Domus*, esp. 702 (1989); 731 (1991): "*In Giappone le città si conservano fiorenti metabolizzando massicce dosi di 'ricambio architettonico' cui sembrano saldamente indifferenti; in Europa le città sembrano sempre più indisponibili a rimettere in discussione il loro stratificato carattere storico limitando al minimo indispensabile i nuovi apporti di architettura.*"

[9] See Fulvio Irace, *Ca' Brütta*, Rome, 1982; and the rich pictorial survey of twentieth-century Milanese architecture in Annegret Burg, *Novecento milanese, I novecentisti e il rinnovamento dell'architettura a Milano fra il 1920 e il 1940*, Milan, 1991, esp. pp. 49ff. (German edition: Annegret Burg, *Stadtarchitektur Mailand 1920-1940*, Basel-Berlin-Boston, 1992.)

Architecture 1984-1995

Exhibition Designs for "The Treasures of San Marco"

exhibition centers:
Grand Palais, Paris, France; Römisch-Germanisches Museum, Cologne, Germany; British Museum, London, United Kingdom; Metropolitan Museum of Art, New York, USA; Los Angeles County Museum of Art, Los Angeles, USA; Dallas Museum of Art, Dallas, USA; Art Institute of Chicago, Chicago, USA; Palazzo del Quirinale, Rome, Italy; Palazzo Reale, Milan, Italy; and Palazzo Ducale, Venice, Italy
client:
Ing. C. Olivetti & SC. Spa, Ivrea (Turin), Italy; the exhibition was organized by the Olivetti Cultural Relations Board in conjunction with the Procuratoria di San Marco, la Réunion des musées nationaux, Paris and the Metropolitan Museum of Art, New York

"The design concept was based on the fact that the same items were to be transported to several different exhibition locations.
The solution adopted was to create a display consisting of a series of 'containers' which would be identical each time they were set up. Thus a special case was designed in the form of a glass pyramid, supported by four columns. The lighting was of primary importance: while the source of the light itself was concealed, the value and rarity of the item on show was so carefully highlighted that the glass almost became imperceptible.
The overall effect was to create an atmosphere of penumbra round the unique character of each strikingly highlighted object and at the same time provide all-round close visibility.
The exhibition was inaugurated at the Grand Palais, Paris, before going on to the Römisch-Germanisches Museum, Cologne, the British Museum, London, the Metropolitan Museum, New York, the Los Angeles County Museum of Art, the Dallas Museum of Art, the Art Institute of Chicago, the Palazzo del Quirinale, Rome, the Palazzo Reale, Milan and the Palazzo Ducale, Venice." (E. Ranzani, *Mario Bellini Architetture*, Electa, Milan, 1988).

Ermanno Ranzani

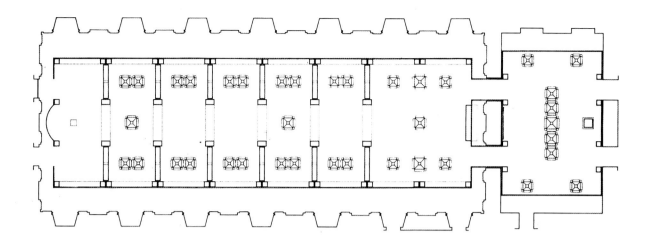

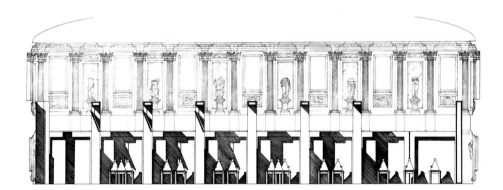

Plan, longitudinal section and cross section of the Caryatid Room.

Views of the exhibition and display panels.

location:
Via Kuliscioff, Milan
client:
Scotti Immobiliare Spa, Milan
project:
from 1984
executed:
1986-88

One or two things I know about Mario Bellini

Remarks on the PL3 and PL4 buildings in Via Kuliscioff in Milan

For objective reasons, I can't offer an impartial and therefore legitimate critique of Mario Bellini's architecture. Our joint experience editing *Domus* for six years brought us too close together both in terms of intellectual outlook and friendship for me to make an unbiased assessment.

I can, however, try to mention just a few things I think I know about his architecture which has stimulated me into various lines of thought. For example, those buildings in Via Kuliscioff. Or to be more precise, the precast panel, the basic unit forming the skin and defining the volumes and surfaces.

This precast reinforced concrete panel was designed to a 120 x 60 cm module. The surface has a strong three-dimensional pattern, similar to the texture of stonework on grand old palaces. But this is allusion, not imitation. For even the least attentive observer will have no doubts that this panel belongs to the contemporary world.

But is it quite true to say that the panel on the Via Kuliscioff buildings is entirely a product of our times? Look at the powerful, elegant relief pattern and the sophisticated handling of the surface where the perimeter ridges are smooth, while the internal sections are sandblasted, thus highlighting the colour and the grain of the marble grit mixed with concrete. The care over the pattern, the material and the surface effect seem almost to be reminiscent of the past – an historical legacy miraculously survived to the present.

And this is what I find so interesting and exciting about his architecture: even though he conforms entirely to today's requirements, embracing the various practical trends, respecting technical constraints and fully exploiting resources, he never forgets the richness and nobility of historic architecture. But without being backward-looking, or trying to re-create artificially economic and productive conditions now inevitably things of the past. Instead, firmly rooted in the present, he skilfully exploits the past's lessons to make a more attractive and dignified world.

It might be claimed that the buildings in Via Kuliscioff, or at least the fronts, herald industrial design's entry into the realm of architecture. That may well be the case, but it's nothing to get upset about. On the contrary, it seems a logical and intelligent move. For if architecture (or rather, some kinds of architecture) has now become an industrialized product, then it is only right

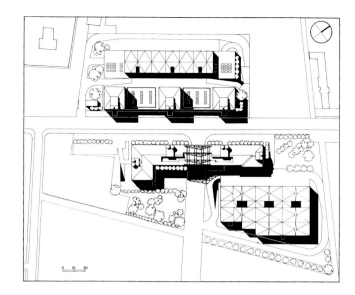

that this industrialized product should be designed exactly like any other mass product. The normally amorphous precast concrete panels must thus be endowed with the same culture and aura as cars and all other mass-produced items for human consumption.

It might be objected that the buildings in Via Kuliscioff consist of nothing more than superficial decoration. That might also be true, if superficial refers to the surface of the building. But that's nothing outrageous either. Because today's architecture (or rather some kinds of architecture) has become 'skin and skeleton' architecture, though not in the way intended by Mies van der Rohe. Especially in new speculative office developments, volumes are dictated by the need to maximise real-estate profits; the load-bearing structures are restricted to the construction methods available on the market; and the interiors are the outcome of the maximum use of space and most economic fixtures and furnishings. The area for the architect's design ideas has been cut back to the skin of the building, that is, the facade. This is all very regrettable, but it is the reality professionals have to face. And it is no good trying to ignore it: for every architect who turns down a job there is always another waiting to take his place. Instead, it is worth making the best of the situation for the sake of the ultimate aim of the project, i.e. to convey culture. And in far from easy conditions but with extremely effective results, this is precisely what Mario Bellini has achieved in Via Kuliscioff. Any critical comment concerning the buildings PL3 and PL4 should consider how strongly they stand out in the depressing and muddled suburban setting surrounding them; it should analyse the design rigour of these new works and praise their simplicity and building intelligence. But as I said, this is not a proper critique. It is just one or two things that I think I know about an architect who, from his precise, whole-hearted knowledge of the contemporary scene, almost surreptitiously manages to distil the qualities of a tradition. And although aware that tradition can't be reproduced, he resolutely refuses to give it up for lost.

Vittorio Magnago Lampugnani

Typical floor plan.

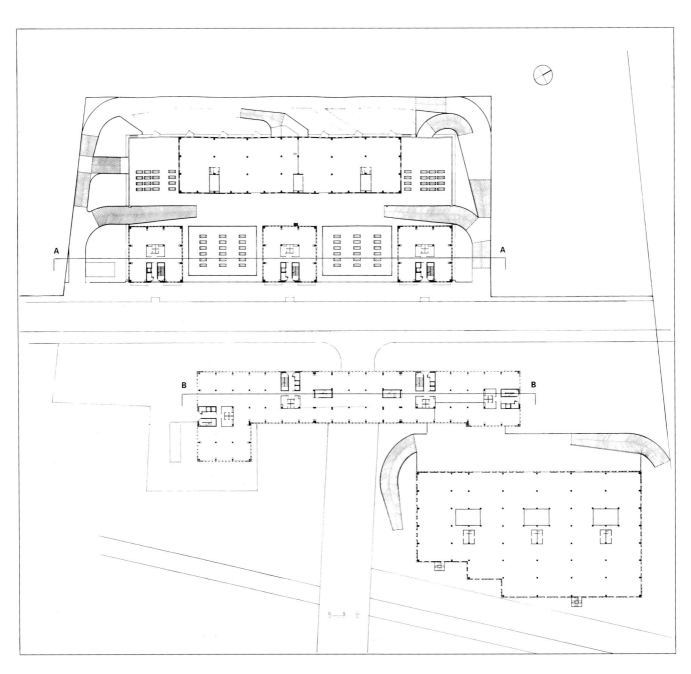

A   A

B   B

Main street fronts and sections AA
and BB.

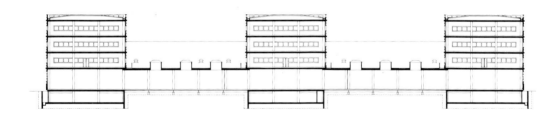

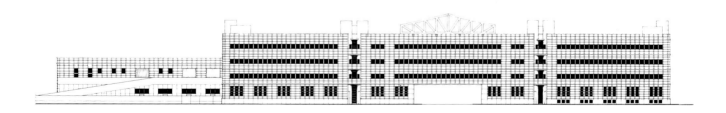

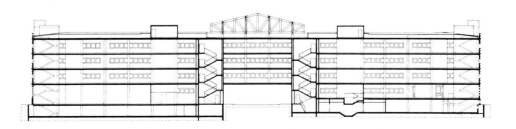

Building details of in-fill panelling.

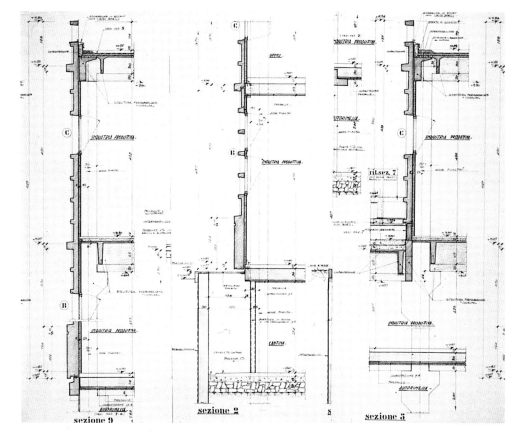

opposite page
Elevation and section of tower-stairs-lifts.

Views of entrance to a tower
containing stairs and lifts.

following pages
*The large portal with the street
through the complex.*

Detail of a corner of the building.

Facades on Via Kuliscioff.

**Offices and Landscaping for the
Cassano D'Adda Thermoelectric
Power Station
Cassano D'Adda (Milan), Italy**

location:
Cassano d'Adda (Milan), Italy
client:
Azienda energetica municipale
Milano (Aem)
project:
1985
executed:
1989-90

"Mario Bellini's design emphasizes this already sharply connoted context by introducing a decisive 'sign' into the rural landscape. The architect has built an 'inhabited wall', whose dual purpose is to delimit the industrial zone and to enhance the relation between the built-up area and the land around it, while meeting functional needs. The project in fact springs from the urgent requirement to protect the surrounding – and particularly the inhabited – area, from the noise pollution caused by a number of particularly noisy plants. This need provided an opportunity to carry the metaphor of the wall to its extreme consequences as the limit between two heterogeneous systems: the town and the factory, the place of residence and the place of work. Only partially completed, the building powerfully conveys the idea of a 'large fragment', whereas its mainly horizontal development reinforces its presence as a sign in the landscape. The context is thus reorganized as the sign is conjugated in an image rich in allusions to the themes of the architectural debate within the Modern Movement. The 'rational' contents of that debate are enunciated in redesigned built images through a reliance on a – again symbolic – use of materials such as washed gritstone or coloured blocks. In particular, the treatment of materials is primarily defined

at an historical level, where a connection is established between modern materials (prefabricated concrete blocks) and finishing techniques traditionally used for brick facings (the sand-blasted unfaced surface) so that a sort of possible dialogue is created with the brick construction in front.
The figure of a limit, the structure's horizontal development is emphasized by using various courses of small blocks. The result is a design that explicitly renounces all 'machine worship' or any exaltation of technology so as to create a place of mediation between the factory and the surrounding area. The dichotomy between the artificial and nature, however, is reflected in the planned vegetal facing of the building ultimately to be transformed into a 'green rampart', in an even more radical renunciation of architectural language's claims over the world. The intrusion in the landscape is therefore reduced to the discretion of a 'sign', later to be concealed or, to take the metaphor to its logical consequences, to be transformed by nature into new nature."
(F. Moschini, *Domus*, no. 722, December 1990).

Francesco Moschini

Site plan.
1. Office building.
2. 'Green' barrier.

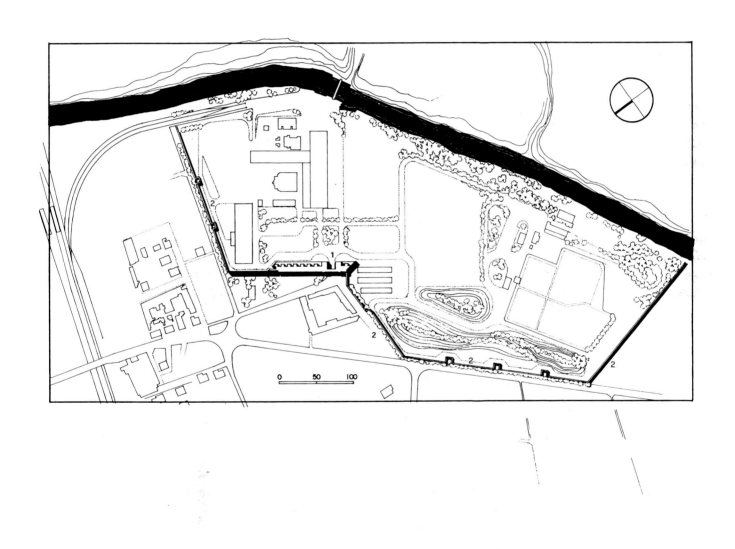

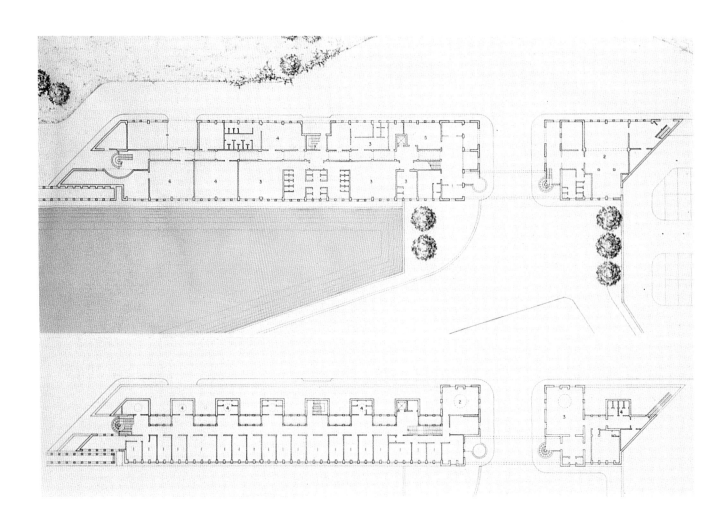

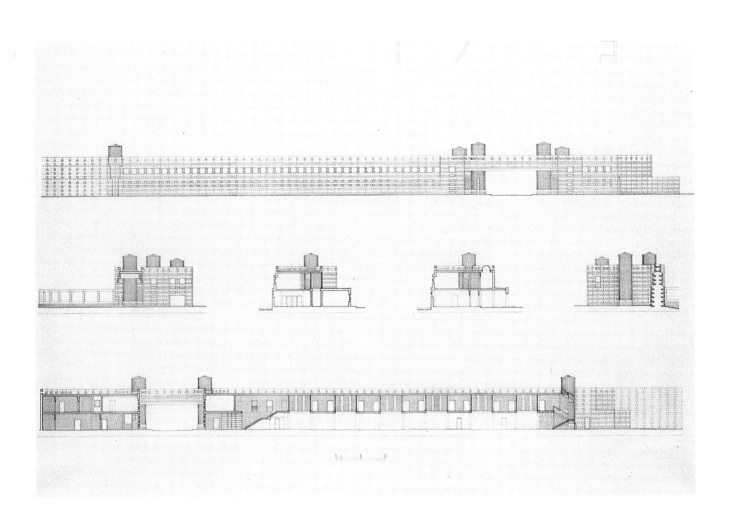

Entrance.

*Elevation of the office building
and the 'green barrier'.*

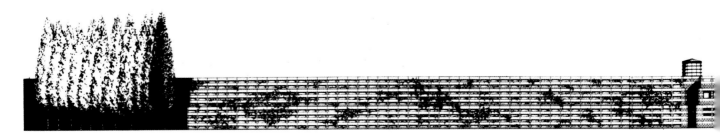

Interior views.

Competition for the new National Theatre
Tokyo, Japan

location:
Honmachi, Shibuya ward, Tokyo,
Japan
competition organizers:
Ministry of Construction, Japan
project:
1986

"The area

Some critical features and aspects of the chosen site must be taken into careful consideration in the design concept.

1. The area is closed on two sides: on the north it is limited by very low-slung buildings, and on the east by some taller, more sparsely spread unsightly constructions.

2. The other two sides are in direct contact with the city: the west side faces onto a shopping street where the buildings are scattered and small in size; the south side opens onto a large-scale avenue, somewhat oppressed by an overhead highway.

3. The area is large enough to contain all the specified functions but not so extensive as to permit the spacious planning that such an important project deserves.

In order to create a harmonious and meaningful relationship with the surrounding area, as well as satisfying the obvious requirements of access and circulation, the project had to fully take into account this unusual urban context.

The design therefore deliberately sets out to involve the entire area, facing strategically outwards on all four sides, with the aim of stimulating, rather than passively undergoing, any future urban developments in the environs.

The design

The design is organized around a central courtyard, open towards the south. The theatre buildings and their related bulky installation and service structures are concentrated to the north, while to the east and west, two long, arcaded wings enclose the large sloping square in front of the theatres. This solution provides an overall view of the entire complex, emphasized by the arrangement of the axes of the three theatres and the two wings. On the west side the complex is linked to the city by a horizontal, arcaded structure, providing the necessary transition to the smaller scale of the adjoining shopping area.

The inner part of the other horizontal arcaded structure on the opposite west side runs along the sloping edge of the square. Both the arcaded wings physically link the sloping square to street level and act as channels for the flow of people arriving either from the subway stations or by private and public transport, orienting them towards the two entrances to the shared theatre lobby.

Lastly, the theatre buildings themselves form a castellated backdrop to the square, and this, together with the two wings, turns the urban setting into an impressive theatrical scene, a sort of theatre of theatres, or theatre of the city, where the buildings occupy the stage-square and citizens become the actors.

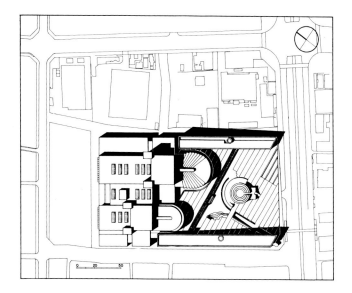

The theatres

Each of the three theatres is designed to express its unique character as an architectural body and 'machine' for performances.

The restless mass of dramatic variously-sized towers and of the side-stages provide a strong contrast to the open spaces of the stalls and galleries, where the arrangement of volumes and the finishing express externally the different typological features of the interiors.

The theatres – places for representations – are thus themselves transformed into the representation of various architectural types.

The architect who designs a theatre is confronted with centuries of history. And tradition has not been ignored here, but revisited with a shrewd eye to the now indispensable technological innovations of our time.

Thus in the large *opera theatre* the layout of the so-called 'Italian-style' theatre can be recognized in the overall form of the building and in the memory of the circle boxes, transformed into more suitable comfortable galleries offering a better view of the stage.

The return to an extensive use of wood for the balconies and the caisson ceiling helps to create a magical aura akin to that of a musical instrument. In the *middle theatre*

the single large hemisphere alludes to the typology of the classical Greek theatre, but flexible positioning of the various functions and the seating means it is also a highly innovative structure.

The *little theatre* draws on the concept of Gropius' Total Theatre – the ultimate in experimental theatres. Its central-plan structure is also visible at square level, where it emerges as a small open-air theatre." (M. Bellini, from the Project Report).

Mario Bellini

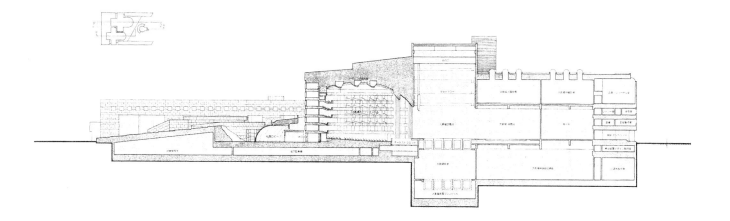

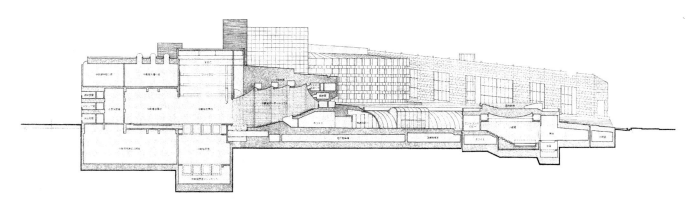

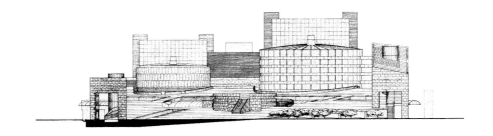

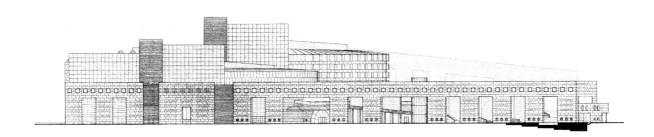

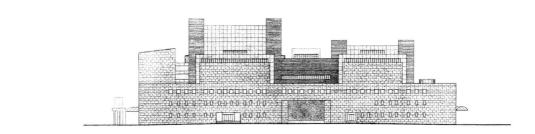

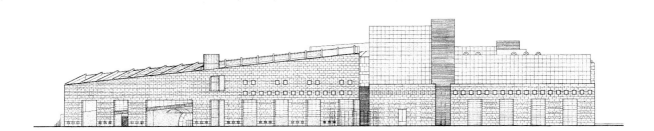

Model views.

following pages
Perspective view of the square.

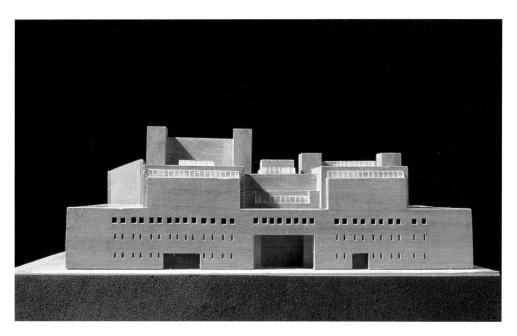

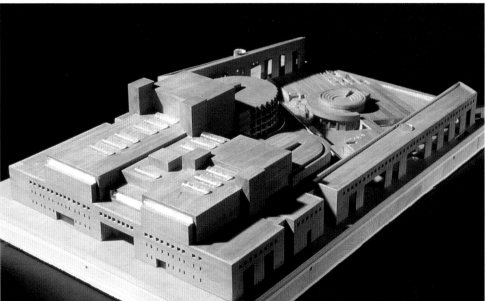

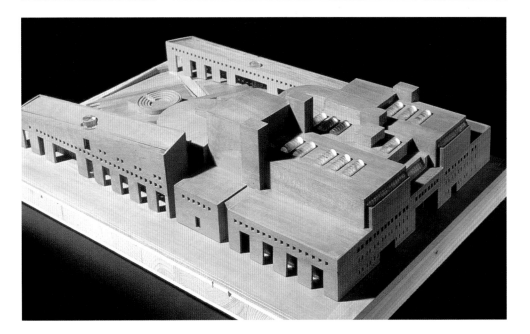

location:
Palazzo dell'Arte, Milan, Italy
organizer:
Ente Autonomo Triennale
di Milano
date:
18 January – 23 March 1986

"In the early decades of the twentieth century, in Europe and the United States, all aspects of designing the home were basically controlled by one professional figure: the architect.

Many of the important – and more especially the revolutionary – developments and ideas in contemporary furnishing were due to the up-and-coming names in the field of architecture – figures as varied as Mackintosh, Le Corbusier, Mies, Aalto, Wright, Rietveld, Hoffmann, Gropius, Wagner, Chareau, Behrens, van de Velde and Loos. At the time they believed it was only natural for an architect to deal with all aspects of the 'home' and occasionally went so far as to design cutlery, door handles, carpets, clothes, jewellery and even – as in the case of Le Corbusier – cars.

In the period after the Second World War, the neo-capitalist reorganization of society, production and intellectual activity spelled out the end for the *Gesamtkunstwerk* utopia; but with the demise of the all-round designer, a fertile cross-disciplinary synergic situation was also lost. While the neopositivist approach to industrial design began to take root, the architecture schools and faculties retreated into narrower academic confines. Thus having lost its unity, 'home design' verged on total disintegration into a host of professional specializations.

Contemporary architectural theory, whether critical or historical, too often ignores or neglects this awkward but crucial subject, dismissing it as a minor aspect of interior architecture, or distractedly confusing it with the sub-culture of 'furnishings' in an initially naive but subsequently treacherous attempt to short-circuit its historical depth or cultural value with the pretext of the need for industrial design. Especially outside Italy – still a unique example of continuity in the great 'modern' European tradition – there are clear signs that architecture is becoming separated from its 'interiors' and that the 'interiors' are alienated from their general architectural framework. Those kinds of figures who enlivened the architectural scene at the beginning of the century with their breadth of vision are now a rarity and contemporary interior design is lacking in creative flair and quality. Moreover, even in its attempts to establish a relationship with the city and with history, at times architecture itself is 'in danger' of being reduced to an 'architecture of exteriors'. Given this academic and professional context, the exhibition held at the seventeenth Triennale of Milan, *Il progetto domestico*, is of particular importance. Focused on the state of knowledge about 'home-living', this wide-ranging exhibition makes a new attempt to relate the

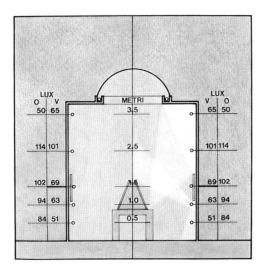

'prototypes' of today to the archetypes of western 'home design' by retracing how life-styles have developed from the origins of the Modern Movement." (M. Bellini, *Domus*, no. 671, April 1986).

Mario Bellini

"The exhibition design is organized round a main historical collection marked off by the dome lights of the Palazzo della Triennale. In addition, there are side 'chapels' (rooms dedicated to specific themes) and 'cloisters' housing the installations of guest designers and arranged in a dialectical relation with themes dealt with in various sections. These three areas: the nave, the side chapels and the cloisters, are distinguished by three different relations with Muzio's original building.

The nave is formed by closing off and highlighting the pattern made by the dome lights with walls rising to just twenty centimetres from the beams above. The side chapels, situated in the area under the shed roofs, are lower and narrower than the central gallery and have barrel-vault ceilings. In this case the structure of the Palazzo dell'Arte is no longer visible. When you reach the installations of the twenty-six guest architects, however, the Palazzo reappears as if it were 'external', like an open space.

The lighting of the historical section posed a special problem. The materials to be displayed consisted mainly of drawings and paintings requiring very precise quantities of light. In the case of drawings, including gouache and watercolours, the lighting could not exceed 60 lux horizontally. A system of reflected light falling from above was adopted so as to provide the right amount of perfectly diffused light without any penumbra effects.

The central gallery skylights covered by suitable curtains and the barrel vaults of the side-rooms functioned as reflectors diffusing light from the luminous strip beneath.

The system of curtaining adopted deserves close attention: the curtains consist of two pieces of material joined together – one side blacking out, the other reflecting – thus also making it possible to regulate the amount of natural lighting."
(M. Romanelli, *Domus*, no. 671, April 1986).

Marco Romanelli

Plan of the exhibition.

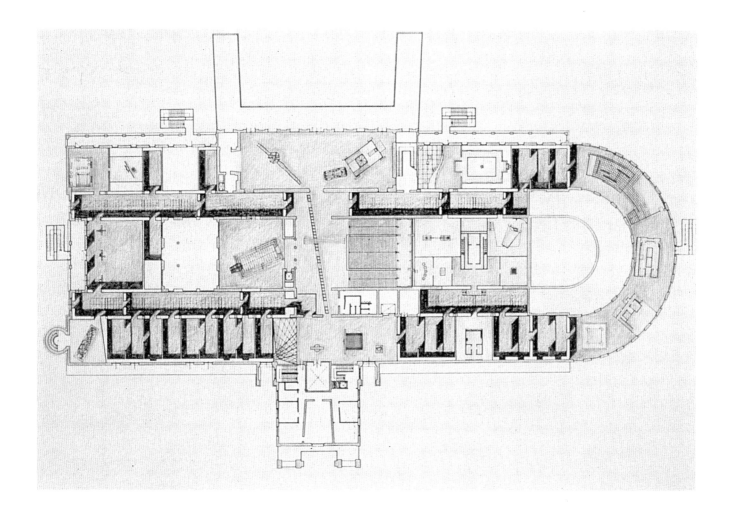

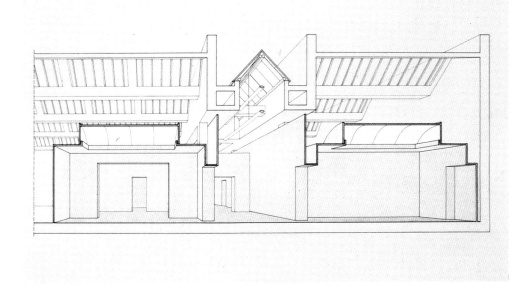

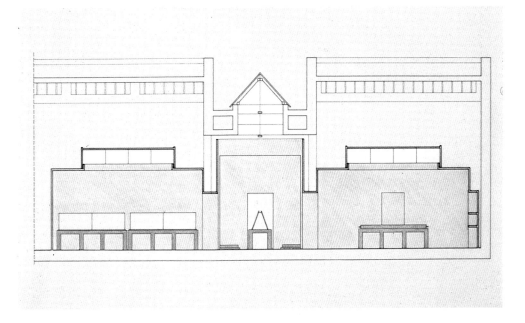

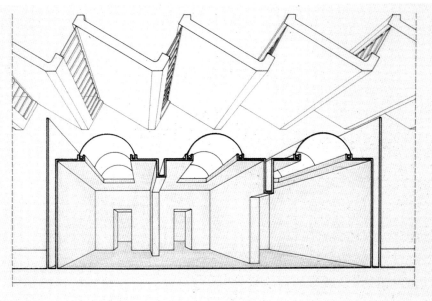

Circulation spine.　　　　The small exhibition rooms.　　　　following pages
The exhibition entrance - the 'box
of the soul'.

1986-90

**Villa Erba International Congress
and Exhibition Center, Cernobbio
(Como), Italy**

location:
Villa Erba Park, Cernobbio
(Como), Italy
client:
Villa Erba SpA, Cernobbio (Como),
Italy
project:
from 1986
executed:
1987-90

"... Bellini adopted a number of guiding principles for his design that have shaped the architecture, the plan and the response of the building to its landscaped setting. Firstly, the new buildings defer to the original Villa rather than attempt to compete with it. They are set some distance away, allowing the Villa to maintain its relationship with the landscape, and adopt a low, restrained profile. In their form they take something of the character of the conservatory and greenhouse structures that nineteenth-century gardeners might once have erected in the grounds of such houses, albeit on a larger scale. But these buildings are not facsimiles. Instead, they paraphrase the glass curves of the originals, offering just enough of the idea of a greenhouse to make the Center feel as if it belongs in this garden.

The other aesthetic system determining the design is one of ordered but subtle classicism; the swooping glass walls' transverse passages built in concrete blocks terminate naturally in a line of solid porticoed entrances surmounted by a tympanum, the successful consequence of the iron and glass pitched roof. The Villa Erba site is roughly rectangular, with the narrow side facing the lake. The villa is in the corner nearest the lake, and the new complex backs away from it into the opposite corner near the road. The two

wings nearest the villa tactfully refrain from aligning with its facades.

The exhibition center was carefully positioned to avoid the destruction of trees on the site, and in its choice of materials and finishes shows respect for its setting, blending rather than contrasting with it. The real mass of the building is played down by the fact it is organized into a grouping of smaller elements. These add up to a coherent whole, but do not read as one gigantic object.

There is an underlying order, both in the use of materials, which displays a coherent and persuasive logic throughout, and the way in which the plan unfolds. At play here is the successful use of a hierarchy of design elements, irradiating from the circular center out towards the wings. The juxtaposition of the solid and the transparent involves an extensive use of glazed walls in the exhibition rooms, offering views of Lake Como and the garden. The effect is to produce not only a fitting neighbour for a fragile fragment of the past in an extraordinary setting but also a highly successful exhibition center in its own right..." (D. Sudjic, *Blueprint Extra*, no. 8, monographic issue, 1993).

Dejan Sudjic

Site plan.
1. The existing villa.
2. The new Exhibition and
Congress Center.

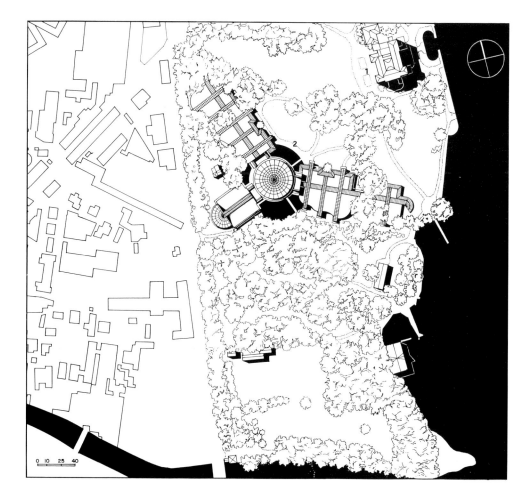

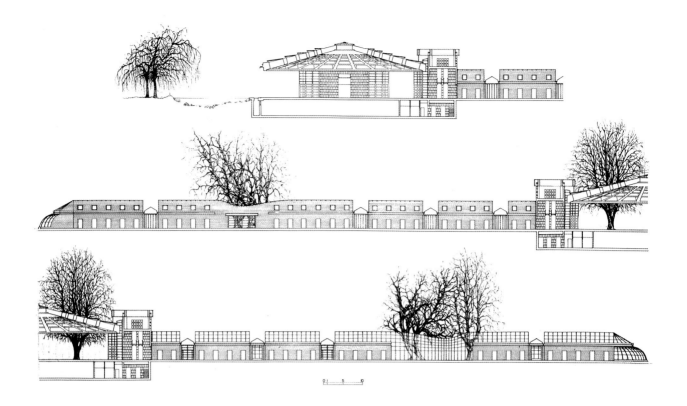

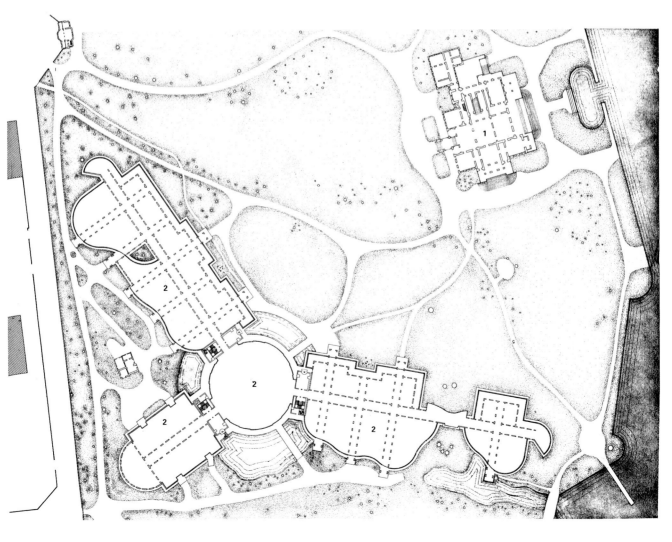

Sections.

Ground floor plan.
1. The existing villa.
2. The new Exhibition and
Congress Center.

Overall view of building and
ground.

Aerial view of the new complex.

Perspective view of the clearing.

The wing on the lake side.

Axonometric of the central
pavilion and part of the three
wings from below.

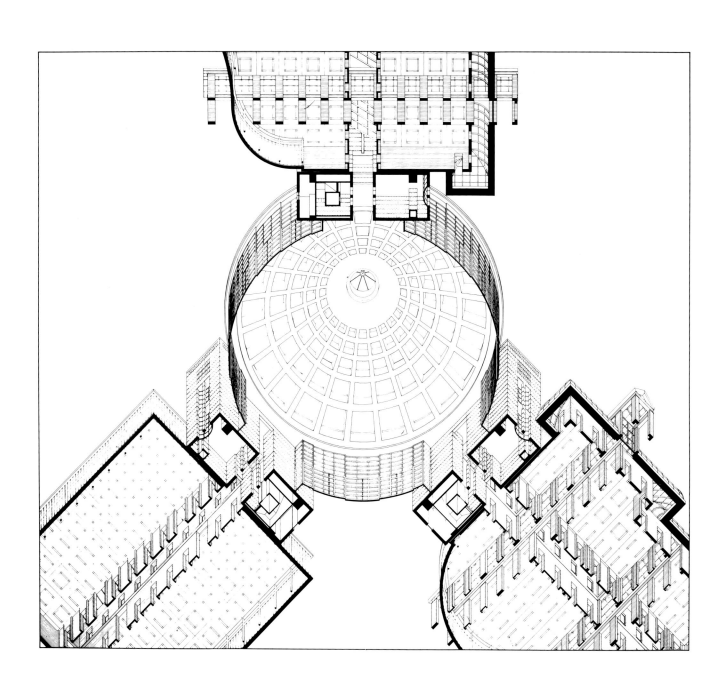

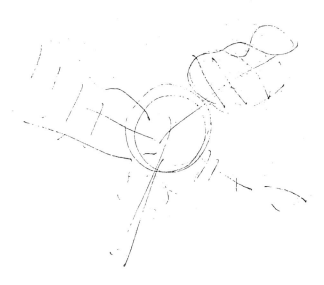

following pages
*Internal view of the central
pavilion and roof.*

Details of the building.

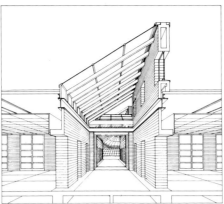
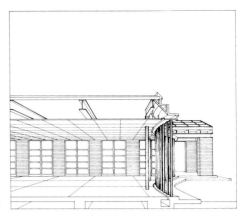

*Southeast wing; axonometric
sections and internal views.*

*Southeast wing; section and view
of central corridor.*

following pages
*South wing with the large plane
tree.*

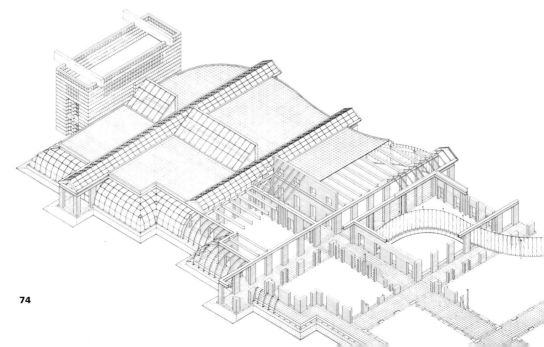

Design for the "Mario Bellini: Designer" exhibition
The Museum of Modern Art, New York, USA

exhibition center:
The Museum of Modern Art, New York, USA
client:
The Museum of Modern Art, New York, USA
date:
24 June -15 September 1987

"The monographic exhibition, 'Mario Bellini: Designer', presented a selection of about fifty works conceived and executed in over twenty-five years of design practice. The New York Museum of Modern Art also invited the architect to design the exhibition itself, thus enabling him to create a coherent framework for variously sized objects, machines and furniture arranged in one space.

The space is organized round the focal point of a semicircular platform with other platforms radiating from it. The circular plan of these platforms intersects with a Cartesian grid of pedestals each supporting an office machine or small object.

The square grid and circular space are linked by a long narrow arcade running diagonally across the exhibition space; this also serves as the entrance." (E. Ranzani, *Mario Bellini Architetture*, Electa, Milan, 1988).

Ermanno Ranzani

The Museum of Modern Art entrance during the exhibition.

Plan of the exhibition design.

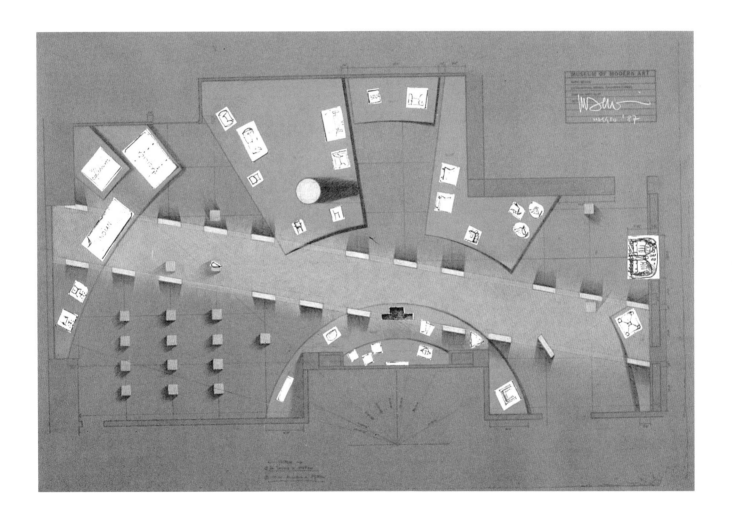

Views of the exhibition.

location:
Godo-cho Hodogaya-ku,
Yokohama, Japan
client:
Nomura Real Estate Dev., Japan
project:
1987
executed:
1987-91

"In this complex – one of the largest private enterprise initiatives of its kind in Japan – public space is conceived as the central 'place' around which the whole master plan is organized.

A circular vaulted arcade-backdrop in an artificial hill, and a paved square-theatre sloping downwards – delimited by a lattice-work rectangular enclosure – are reflected in and overlook a round pool-stage. Converging on this point are the walkways interconnecting the principal areas and buildings as well as linking them to the city.

A mirror for meditation and concentration during intervals between work. A secret landmark, an opportunity for the whole neighbourhood to meet." (M. Bellini, *Obayashi Calendar*, 1994).

Mario Bellini

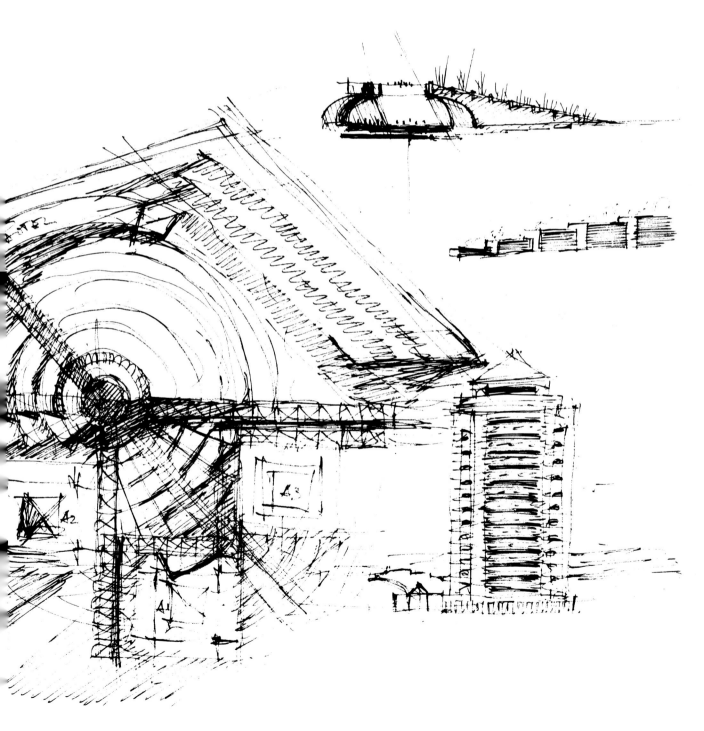

Aerial view of the overall complex.

Site plan.

The central space in the complex.

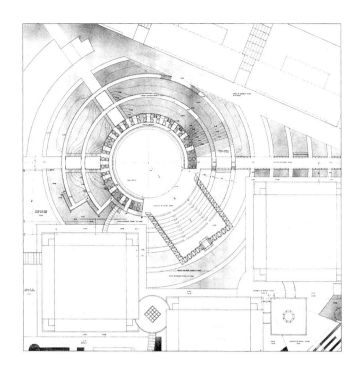

Axonometric and section.   *Central space.*

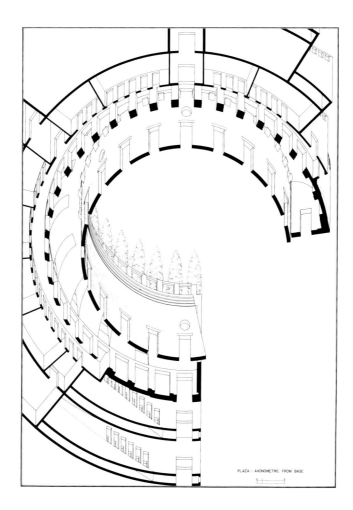

PLAZA · AXONOMETRIC FROM BASE

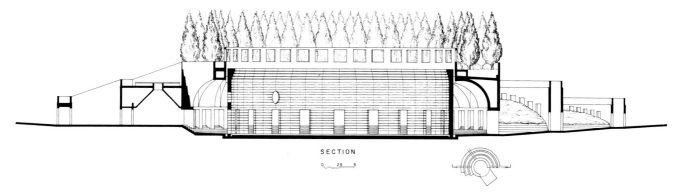

SECTION

0   25   5

Central space.

Views of the corridor round the central space.

location:
Via Scarampo, Milan, Italy
client:
Ente Autonomo Fiera di Milano
project:
1987
executed:
1993-ongoing

"... So the first thing that has to be fairly clearly said is this: here we have one of the first architectural designs that consciously sets out to heal the rift between metaphysics and futurism by constructing a sort of new idiom. This idiom reacts to the only true new phenomenon that has shaped urban projects in recent years: today urban designers seem only to be preoccupied with 'not being dangerous'... In my opinion Bellini has had the courage to shake off this by now almost totally dominant outlook, and indeed he opposes it. I consider this to be an extraordinary, positively 'dangerous' design; dangerous because it eludes any facile descriptions.

We might, for example, list a whole series of things the proposed system of buildings 'is not', and we might say almost nothing about what the structure really is. What we can say for the moment is that this is not a building, nor a system of buildings, but basically an infrastructure. Or rather, it is architecture that falls into the category of infrastructures because it is one of those structures whose vast configuration transcends not only the usual size but above all the usual canons of architecture. An important distinction must be made here, however. We are talking about an 'infrastructure', not a 'megastructure'. Bellini's project has nothing ambiguously 'metabolic' about it, nor is it an 'enlarged form': in looking back to the outsize Enlightenment scale of urban fortifications and city walls, his design seeks to shift a certain idea of Milan from the storehouses of history to the realms of a 'utopia of imagery' deeply permeated with a capacity for 'narrative'...

Bellini's project reacts to this steady loss of 'design' with a sensational occupation of urban space. By translating into 'architectural narrative' the literary writing of negotiation, the project for the Fair Center carries out one of the few operations possible in safeguarding architecture's identity and specific quality. A place of 'material' trade in the city of the 'non-material', Bellini's Fair opposes

Sketch for the facade on Via Scarampo.

the dangers of the 'invisible' and the comfort of the 'finite'. Throughout its seven hundred metres, his project seeks and establishes a precisely circumstantiated dialogue with the context, without being ensnared by it. Two traditions coexist and are radically reinterpreted in the light of the 'newness' of the theme. The first is Italian cities' capacity to grow around large scale works. This also involves almost a vocation for an instructive confrontation between public and private, previously separated in a rigid kind of bipolarism...

Since many Italian buildings stand over the ruins of other periods which are then incorporated as memory, it might not be rash to claim that the Milan of the future may well make this exciting 'remnant' of the hope for a better city one of its grounds for new life. ..." (F. Purini, *Domus,* no. 728, June 1991).

Franco Purini

Site plan.
The new pavilions by Mario Bellini are marked yellow.

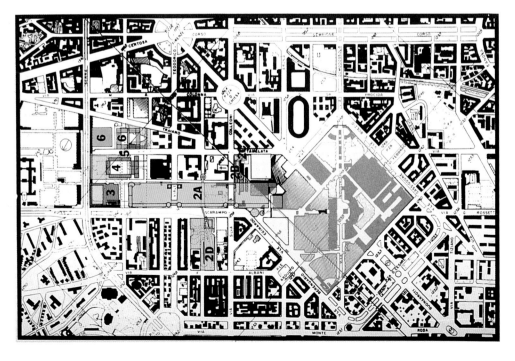

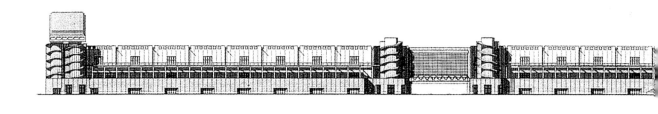

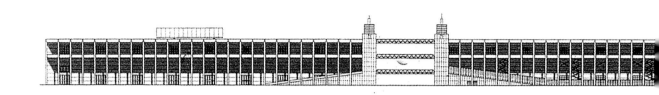

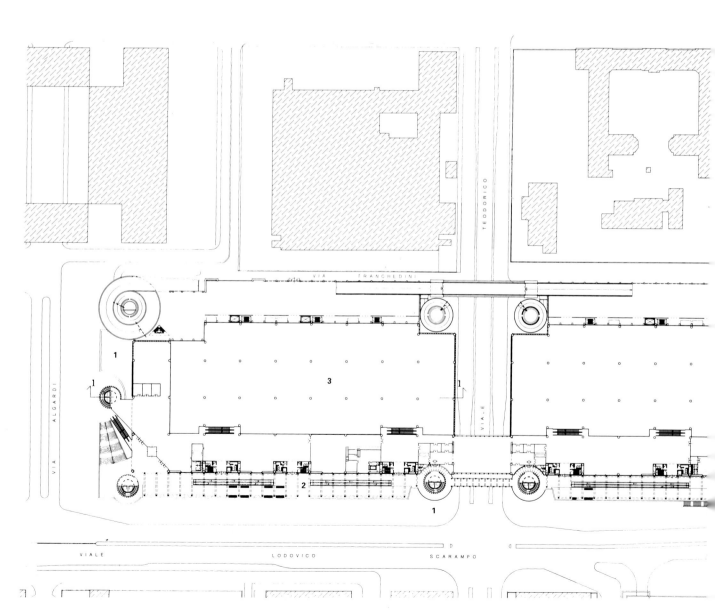

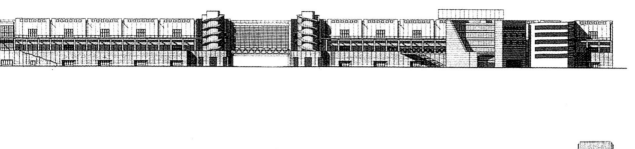

*Elevations on Via Scarampo and
Via Tancredini.*

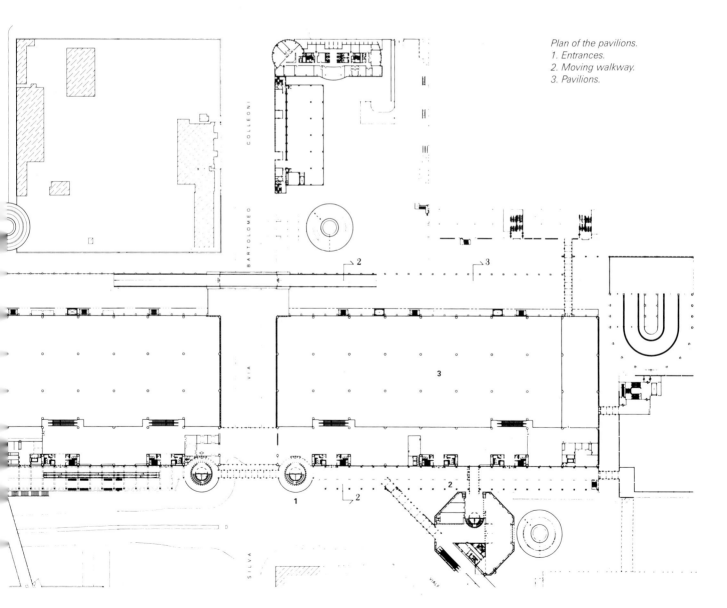

*Plan of the pavilions.
1. Entrances.
2. Moving walkway.
3. Pavilions.*

Design sketch.

Views of the way along Via Scarampo.

following pages
*Photomontage showing one of
the two crossings for Via
Scarampo.*

following pages
*Photomontage of the first floor;
tympanum and the entrance area.*

*Secondary facade and detail of the
entrance portal.*

1988   **Competition for the Ryoma
Sakamoto Memorial Hall
Kochi City, Japan**

location:
Katsurahama Park, Kochi City,
Japan
competition organizer:
Ryoma 150th Anniversary
Projects Executive Committee,
Japan Academic Society of
Construction
project:
1988

"A hypogean vestibule unexpectedly comes out from beneath a circular arcade enclosed in a high open-air volume and facing the center of a pool.
Completely isolated from the outside, only by deliberately crossing a ramp over this empty central space can the visitor reach a terrace flung open towards the ocean.
Lashed by the winds, open to direct conflict with nature atop a steep cliff on the isle of Shikoku, at once lighthouse and ship, the building is a reminder of the eternal voyage of Ryoma Sakamoto."
(M. Bellini, *The Obayashi Calendar*, 1994).

Mario Bellini

"The building stands as a place to the memory of Sakamoto and his deeds. It embodies the whole complex 'memory of the site'. The underlying sacred nature of the place persuaded us to avoid giving the building an image along the lines of the many anonymous spots frequented by tourists; a visit to this place is therefore structured as a meditative and cognitive act, meant to leave a lasting impression on individual and collective experience." (E. Ranzani, *Mario Bellini Architetture*, Electa, Milan, 1988).
The competition theme gave Mario Bellini almost total freedom in choosing typological and linguistic elements. Such freedom meant this project became a grounding for much of the Milanese architect's research: many themes reworked more fully in later years are already clearly outlined here: the metaphysical feel of the great courtyard, the symbolic value of the circle and water, a powerful tension between the elements in the design with its point-form restlessness. In short, what emerges is a sense of the 'dramatic' due to the difficult relation with freedom – an aspect found in many of Bellini's projects.

Ermanno Ranzani

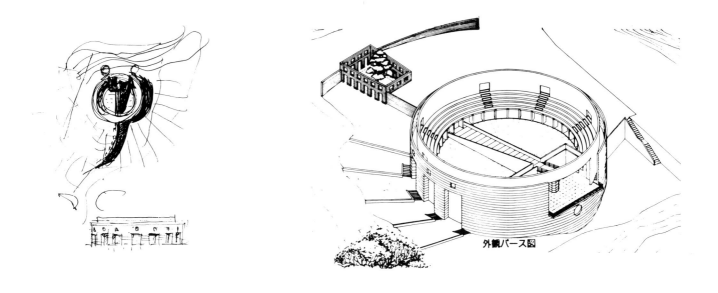

外観パース図

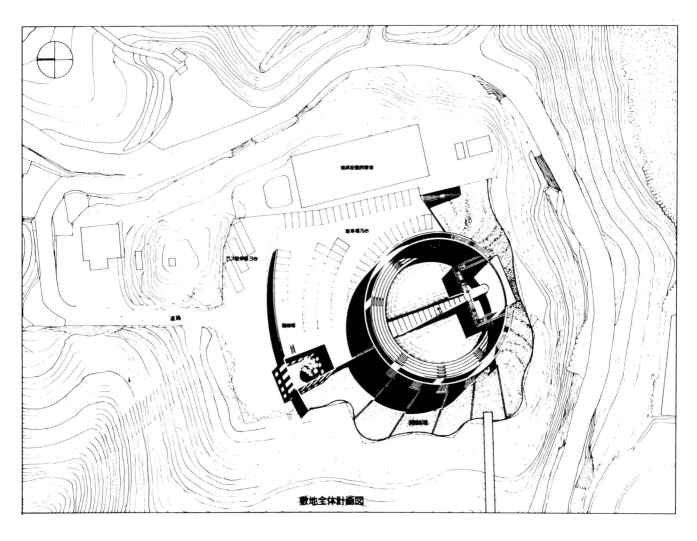

敷地全体計画図

Site plan and axonometric.

Longitudinal section.

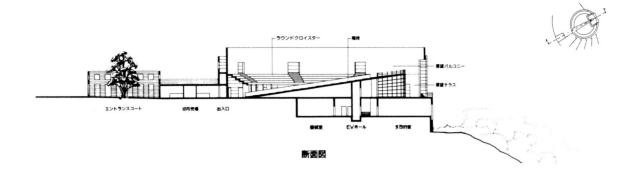

断面図

Plans at various levels.

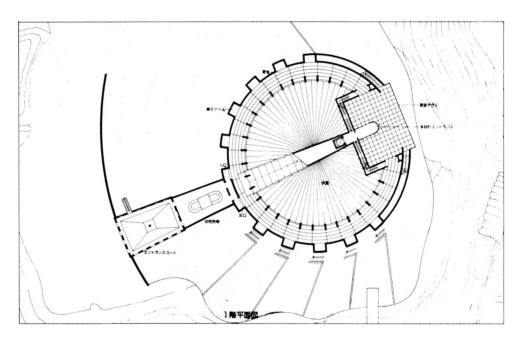

1階平面図

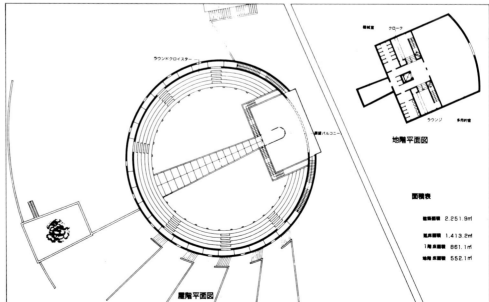

屋階平面図

地階平面図

面積表

建築面積 2.251.9㎡

延床面積 1.413.2㎡

1階床面積 861.1㎡

地階床面積 552.1㎡

113

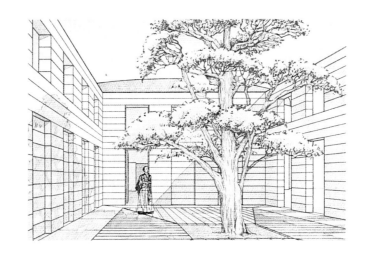

Entrance area.

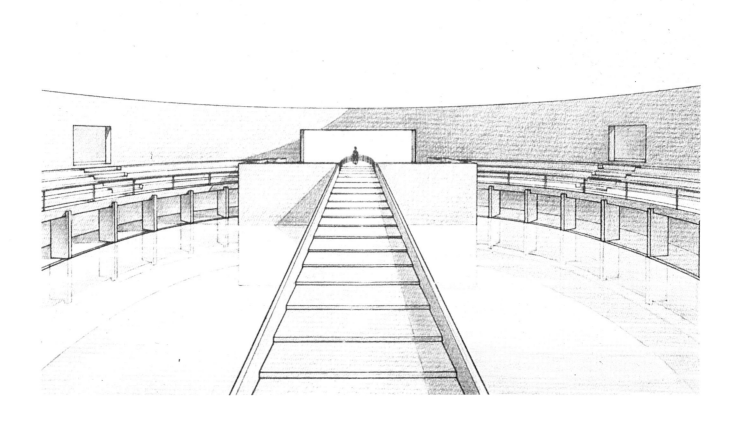

Interior.

location:
25-19 Higashi Gotanda 5-chome,
Shinagawa-ku, Tokyo, Japan
client:
Sowa Shoji Co., Ltd., Tokyo
project:
from 1988
executed:
1989-92

"The site on which Mario Bellini has built the Tokyo Design Center is for me a very familiar one, because I can clearly see its pristine glass dome on the skyline of the Gotanda district from my living-room window. The building is only a five-minute walk from my house, facing the entrance to the subway station I use for commuting to my office. The Tokyo Design Center is a building I will see nearly every day, perhaps a thousand or more times in my life. The irregular, steep site that he was given is in some ways very typical of Tokyo. Topography alone makes design for many sites in Tokyo quite challenging. Often the buildings erected at the foot of a hill end up with a negative, residual space behind them – dark, unused, frequently littered with rubbish. Beyond the problem of topography, however, Bellini has dealt with the unusual additional challenge of having a U-shaped site, wrapped round another building whose owner would not sell the land to developers. Thus, the design of the new building had to deal with the exceptional condition of a discontinuous street-frontage – a facade split in two. Having learned of these difficulties, I became interested in keeping an eye on the site under construction, especially when I heard that Mario Bellini had been commissioned to design a large building there. My vigilance was rewarded. His

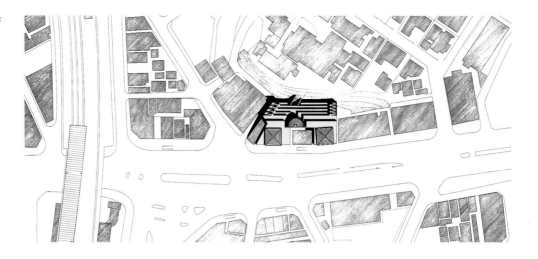

solution for the site is quite ingenious, and though it might be said that he has remained sensitive to the Japanese sense of urban space, at the same time I do not believe there is another building in Tokyo quite like his. It is a canonical principle of city architecture that the representational aspect of a building faces the public domain – which usually means towards a main street – and that the backyard receives more informal treatment. Here, however, Bellini has reversed this principle, making the front facade of the Design Center for the most part non-representational (except for its high, symbolic entryway, which I want to discuss later) while architecturally activating the rear side. In this case it happened to be a brilliant strategy. Since the front facade of the Design Center is inconveniently split in two by a building lodged in between, a representational facade would have had to contend with that building's nondescript curtain-wall facade in the center of the composition. This was a battle that Bellini wisely chose not to fight. His building secludes itself behind a quiet front.

Curiously enough, this strategy of turning a building inside-out is quite consistent with the traditional Japanese townhouse typology. The old wooden townhouses of Japan always had quiet facades (or high, blank walls, in the case of the Samurai estate), while the interior garden was a place of great visual and emotional richness. Historically, this formal diagram for dwelling is related to the Japanese concept of *oku* – spatial depth achieved through the provision of layers, both physical and psychological. By preserving a home's representational core in a place far removed from the public eye (though perhaps not physically distant), by creating an *invisible center* to every dwelling, there emerged a rich mode of living compatible with Japan's high-density society.

What does the Tokyo design Center hold as its innermost core? Nothing less than a splendid inner courtyard, certainly one of the most psychologically interesting spaces in recent Tokyo architecture.

The rear facade is open and active; offices and restaurants deliberately face this canyon-like courtyard in preference to the street. Reciprocal views of the interior, extended terraces, and an episodic ascent of stairs activate the courtyard scenery. By stepping back the rear facade as it faces the cliff, Bellini provides the courtyard with light and air and creates a striking, almost eerie ambience. This wedge-shaped space between balconies and cliff is a strange and memorable space (and as we know, strangeness is the basis of art's power). Row after row of huge flower pots instantly create a surrealistic scene: a steep cascade of red flowers becoming a part of the concrete balusters. This is a spectacle that we Japanese could never conceive – only an Italian, a countryman of the film-maker Fellini, could dream this scene. Here, perhaps more clearly than usual, we see the essential affinity between scene-making and architectural design. What is most memorable in this building in terms of its contribution to the public realm is the large opening that connects the front street to the rear courtyard directly by a massive stair. From the street one perceives only a large opening directing the eye up towards a patch of sky beyond – in itself an unusual scene in densely built-up Tokyo. The intrigue of this opening invites the passer-by to ascend the stairs, even though he has no business within the building. The passage is a narrow, vertiginous space, flanked and articulated by high travertine walls, and it reminds one of stairs leading to some place unknown yet seemingly important. The equestrian sculpture by Mimmo Paladino placed at the top of this stair esplanade heightens the unusual experience of the ascent and suggests further public space beyond. When one turns back from the high point of the stairway, this narrow opening becomes an effective frame for the fragmented space of the city just glimpsed. Thus the opening between front and back here creates a new

place in between that breathes fresh life into two otherwise nondescript spaces. In the evening, when I walk along the front of this building, the quiet facade recedes into darkness, while the illuminated void of the stair passage takes on the character of a positive space, a fragment of cityscape presented out of context. Suddenly the windows and openings of the side walls lend the space a theatrical air, as if to recreate in twentieth-century Tokyo a version of Serlio's stage-set view of the city. The Tokyo Design Center is a considerable contribution to the task of making city life more exciting and rich in experience. It demonstrates that even in a metropolis like Tokyo, there is room for new and imaginative treatment of context and shaping of space. In an age when the metropolis can no longer expect the canonical principles of urban design to hold together, the accumulation of individual and imaginative efforts, such as Bellini's, appears ever more essential to the cause of providing urban dwellers with a high level of spatial experiences and memories." (F. Maki, *Domus*, no. 743, November 1992).

Fumihiko Maki

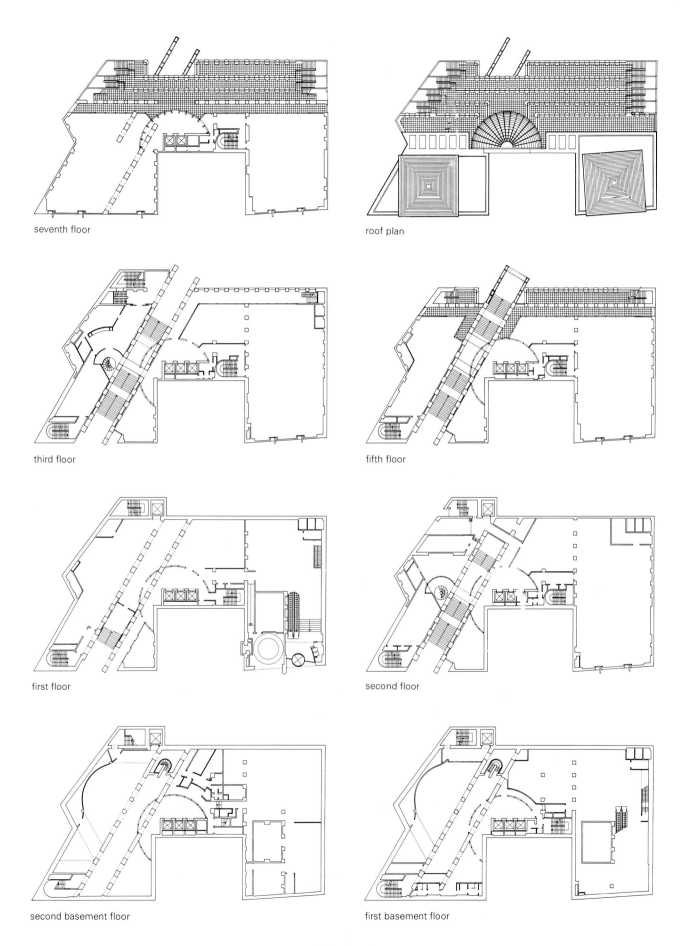

seventh floor

roof plan

third floor

fifth floor

first floor

second floor

second basement floor

first basement floor

The balcony looking towards the garden.

128

Studio model.

The winter garden.

The interior.

location:
Via Madonnina – Via Fiori Chiari,
Milan, Italy
client:
CEID ITALIA – Fondiaria SpA,
Florence
project:
1988
executed:
1991-96

"The design is for two residential buildings in the historic Brera district in the center of Milan. A feature of the area are two bomb-sites from World War II. The project seeks to reconstruct these empty spaces while respecting the pattern and shape of the existing urban fabric. The underlying type elements are those of traditional Milanese building, and especially the use of the characteristic courtyard-staircase-railed balcony (loggia). Suggested by the context and the recent architectural history of the two lots, a number of innovations have been introduced into this basic format, such as the set-back ground floor, the large tree in the courtyard, the vertical cut of the front, and the bay window at the corner of the smaller building." (E. Ranzani, *Mario Bellini Architetture*, Electa, Milan, 1988).

Ermanno Ranzani

"Although Milan is definitely *my* city, my ideal city would perhaps be a mixture of those hundred or so beautiful Italian cities and towns which together embodied the idea of the city in Italy some ten centuries ago before spreading throughout Europe and to the rest of the world.
A city where the huddled houses express a sense of community and give shape to streets, broad and narrow, winding or straight, according to a much more intricate and profound logic than that of traffic flows, a logic whose traces will remain for ever.
A city where houses and monuments, as the lasting expression of citizens' pride, create open places and squares which, with the streets, arcades, fountains and loggias, are the 'place' where public life is expressed – almost theatrically staged – as the necessary counterpoint to individual and private life.
A city not governed by the purely functional logic of traffic, transport and through-roads, of rents and real estate or economic development.
A city which proudly attempts to save the traces and sense of its history, which regards its monuments as an inviolable heritage as it also aspires to change and ensure its continuing vitality." (M. Bellini, *Town and Design*, 1991).

Mario Bellini

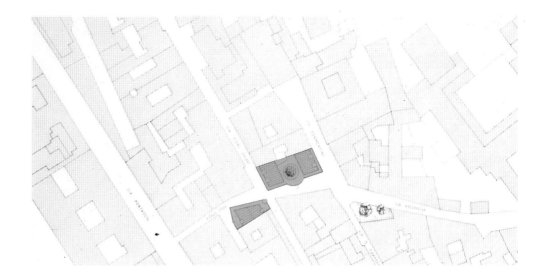

Site plan. Mario Bellini's two projects are marked blue.

Ground floor plans.

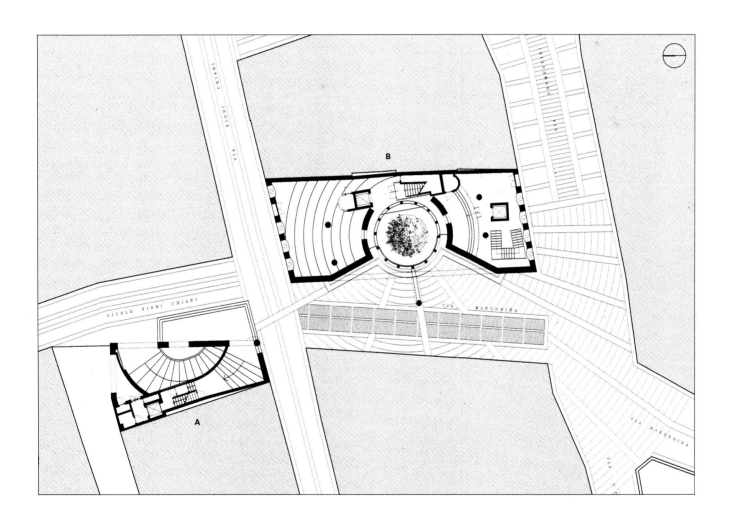

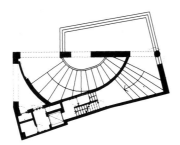

ground floor plan

loft plan

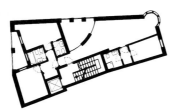

typical plan

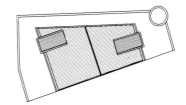

roof-level plan

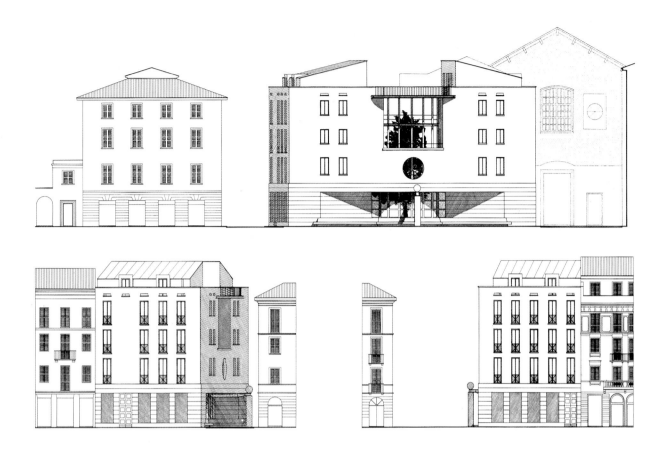

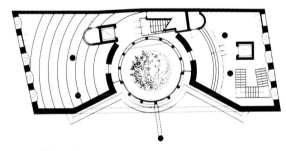

ground floor plan

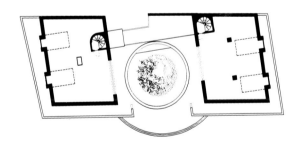

loft plan

typical plan

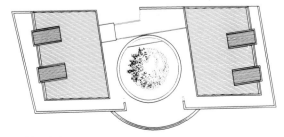

roof-level plan

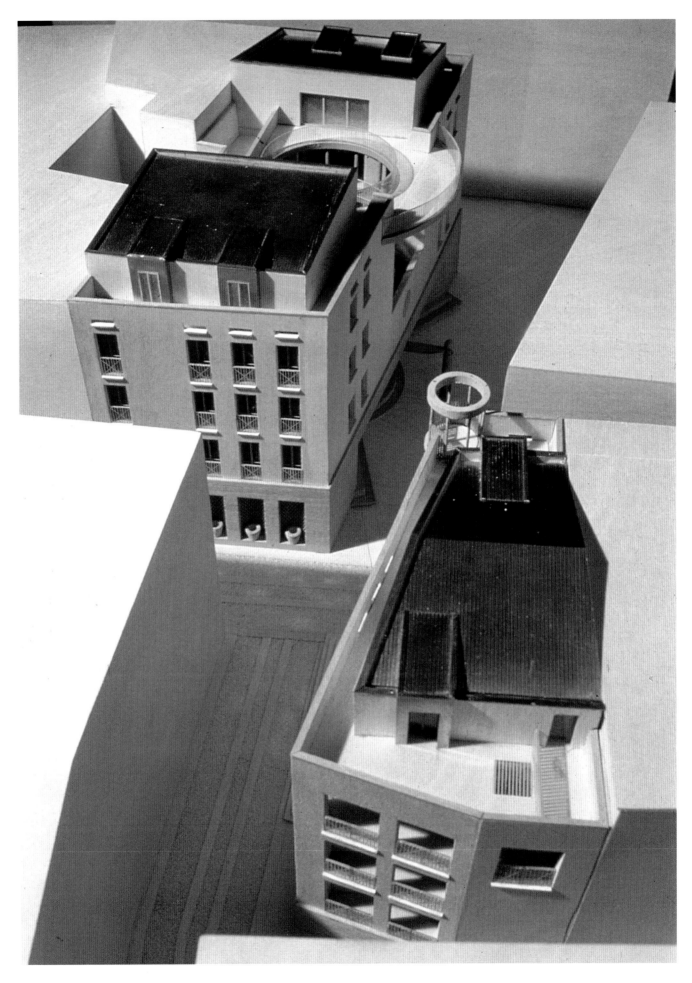

Model of Building A.

Model of Building B.

location:
Via Varese, Milan, Italy
client:
Gyante Srl., Milan
project:
1989-92

** The executed building does not
correspond to the original design
shown here*

The theme of the project is in many ways
similar to that already explored by Bellini
in two buildings in Via Madonnina in
Milan. The courtyard – this time elliptic
in form – is the central idea both in terms
of the careful focus on it, and the way it is
related to the city. Here the courtyard is
no longer an 'inner' space cut off from the
street, but a space open to dialogue with
other urban elements. This approach is
found in some of the finest rationalist
buildings in Milan, such G. Muzio's
design for the Ca' Brütta or the Casa
Rustici in Corso Sempione by G. Terragni.
Bellini goes beyond this kind of research
by giving an increasingly strong identity
to the courtyard space irrespective of the
other built parts in the project. In this
design the powerful compression of the
courtyard by its surrounding volumes
reflects the desire to create a dignified
empty space despite the volumetric needs
imposed by real estate pressures.
And in fact it is probably due to the
complex movements of the market that
the building seems to have turned out
distorted compared to the original design
illustrated here.

Ermanno Ranzani

Design sketch.

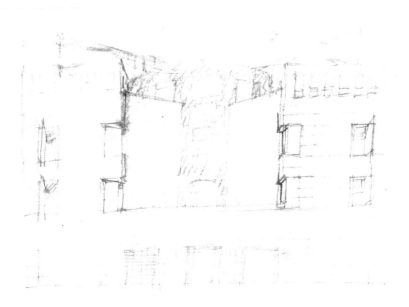

Model: distribution of volumes.

main elevation

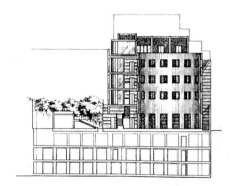

longitudinal section

garden elevation

transverse section

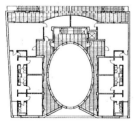

second and third floor

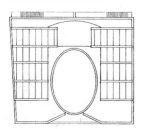

roof plan

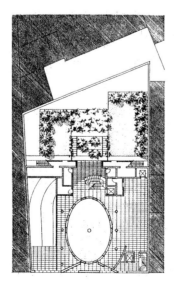

first floor

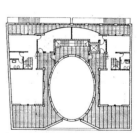

fourth floor

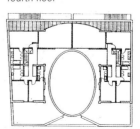

fifth floor

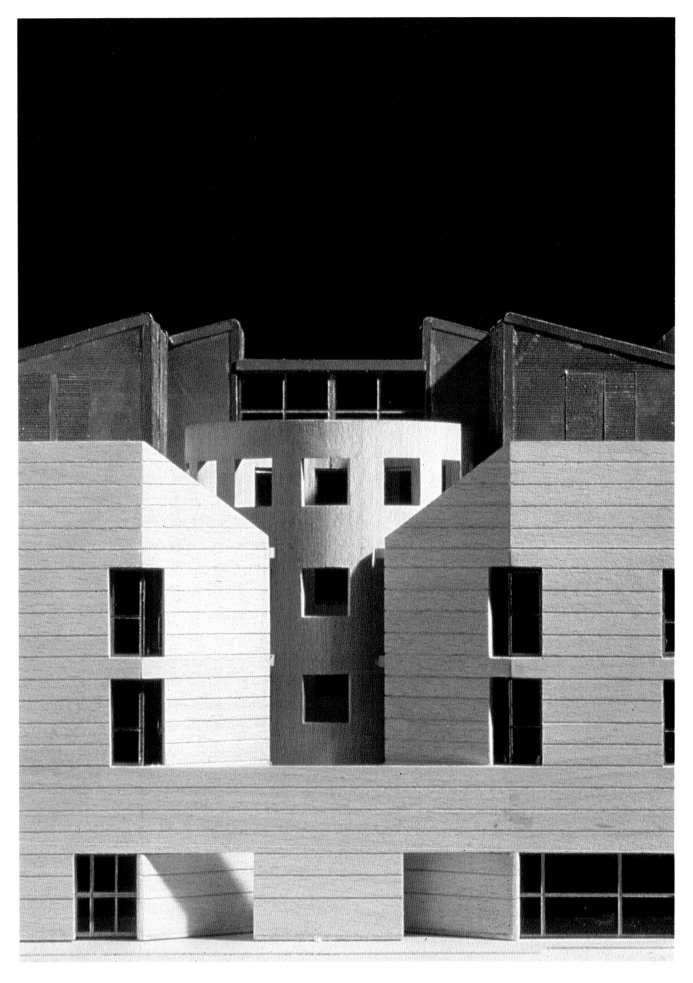

Design for Motorway Service Areas
Italy

location:
various service areas on the
Italian motorway network
client:
Autogrill SpA, Milan
project:
1989
executed:
ongoing

"... The task entrusted to Mario Bellini was to design a building type that could be adapted to various contexts. The Milanese architect has approached this assignment fully aware of the objective limits imposed by the organizational fragmentation of service areas, and of the intrinsic constraints concerning questions of type underlying the project. The design does not deal with the problem of typization. Instead it focuses on a careful architectural and spatial definition of the structure.

The main elements of the building are a large truncated cone and four independent volumes arranged around it. On one side of the cone are two parallelepipeds, one wedge-shaped for the sales sector, and another, in the form of a prism, containing the technical services. On the opposite side, the design is completed by the glazed toroidal volume of the self-service cafeteria unit and by a cube housing the restaurant on the first floor.

The design is distinctive for the sculptural quality of its single units. These tend to be self-contained, even though they are linked by the large truncated cone – the hub of the plan. It is interesting to compare this compositional structure with the – apparently similar – one used in much of Frank O. Gehry's work, where single portions are endowed with a strong

sense of independence, driving the whole composition towards a paratactic juxtaposition in which every element is highly individual. In this work by Mario Bellini the single parts are very precisely and functionally organized, but there is a strong sense of hierarchy preventing the individual parts from becoming totally independent.

On the other hand, the absence of an exact context has led the architect to focus on internal space. But this is dominated by the project's more architectural aspects rather than by a concern to define interiors. In this respect the truncated cone space is strikingly memorable and asserts the design's independence from a given site.

Bellini's service station thus fits in perfectly with his stylistic universe and continues his research into metaphysical space. Despite the encouraging news that perhaps for the first time the problem of designing motorway service areas is now being addressed in architectural terms, more committed critics will hope that this interest will also be extended to devising a more unified approach to all the components of service areas." (E. Ranzani, *Domus*, no. 755, December 1993).

Ermanno Ranzani

Elevations and sections.

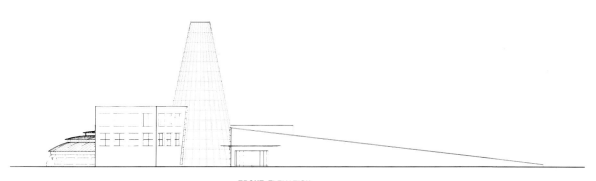

FRONT ELEVATION

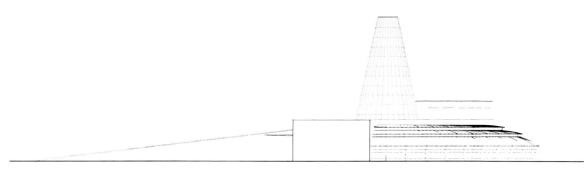

BACK ELEVATION

Ground floor plan.

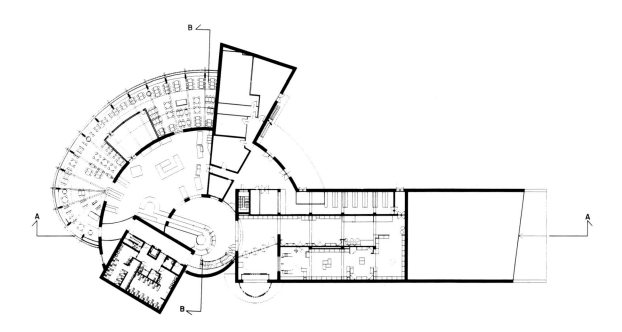

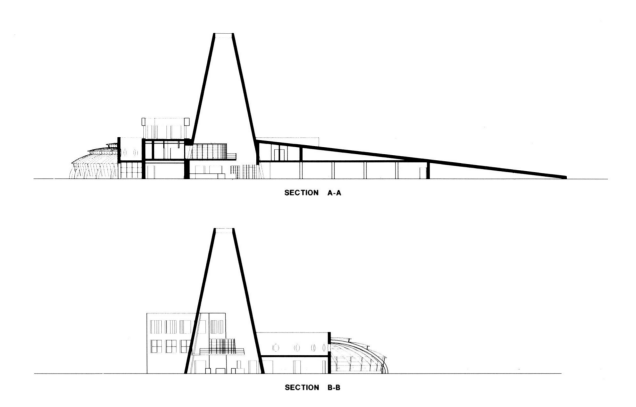

SECTION A-A

SECTION B-B

First floor plan.

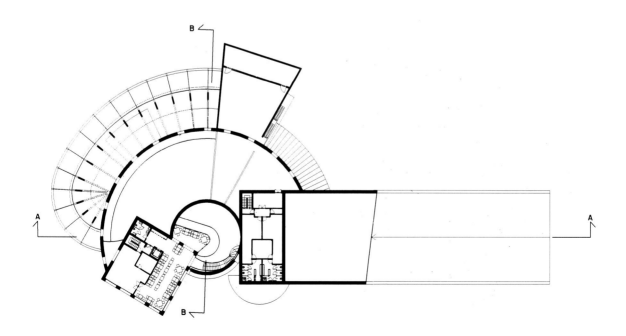

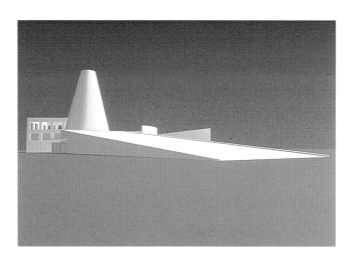

Computer graphic studies.

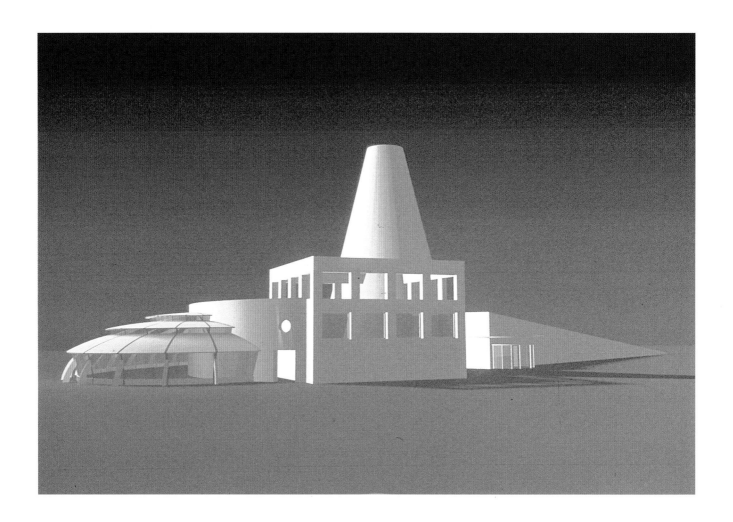

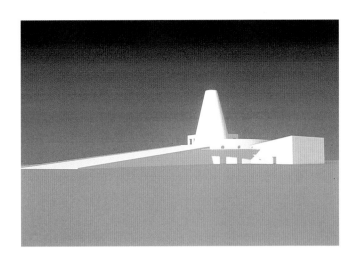

Idea for site plan.

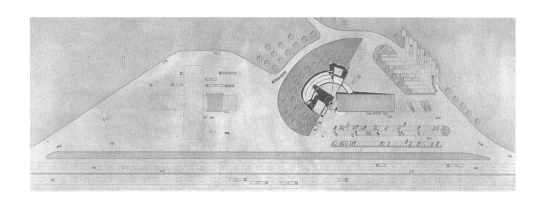

**Competition by invitation for the new
Bayer Italia Center
Milan, Italy**

location:
Milan, Italy
client:
Bayer Italia SpA, Milan
project:
1989

"The Bayer-Portello Center had to provide suitable headquarters for four companies in the Group as well as the mother company, Bayer Italia SpA, which itself consists of nine divisions as well as various central functions and departments. The special way the building is articulated provides a significant response to all these requirements. Each single company or division is located according to the degree of its independence, and has its own identity. At the same time, however, these entities are strategically interdependent or may be connected with others according to hierarchical and functional requirements.

The main entrance on the ground floor is linked to the underground car parks and the general shared facilities situated on the ground and first floors. From here the two towers housing the stairs and lifts provide a centralized system serving the six floors above. These in turn can be subdivided into four independent areas of variable complementary dimensions, each having a 'core' in the four corner towers for their organizational and specialized functions (meeting rooms, recreational areas, toilets and vertical communication between areas on the various floors).

Crossing these matrices of subdivisions for floors and quadrants provides very interesting possible combinations: one or more of the corner towers (or a part) could be identified with a specific company. This in turn may be organized into 'divisions' or 'offices' in the same quadrant but over various floors. Through the vertical 'lines' of the four corner towers, the various companies would then link up with the general management and staff which is to be allocated the top floor. Thus the large portal on the ninth floor connecting the two 'stairway towers' would become, both practically and symbolically, an area for board or joint company meetings and receptions, as well as for the necessary support structures (administration, bathrooms, waiting rooms, bars and catering).

To summarize, a clear distinction has been made between the service areas and the areas served. The former are represented by the series of towers: two form the main vertical lines of communication, while the other four are focal points, connecting the various activities of companies, divisions and functions, providing them with the appropriate infrastructures. However, while the towers are fixed points of reference, the main feature of the areas served is their total flexibility. This has been achieved by using a strictly modular design throughout and completely removing all upright elements from the six structures, which are almost literally 'hung' between the towers.

The programme of building in two phases

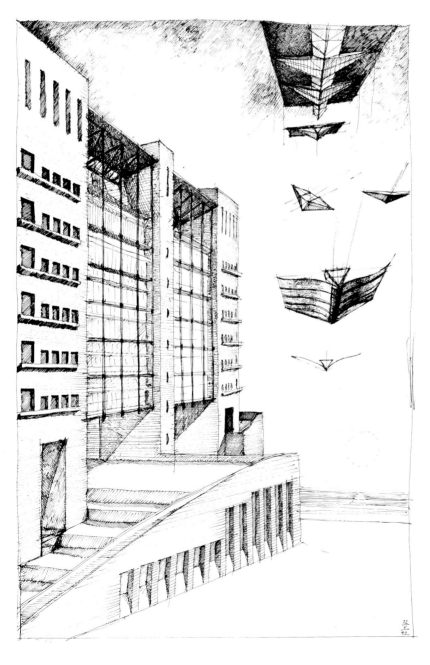

and the break in the buildings at street level caused by Via del Portello made it extremely difficult to find a solution to the complex problems of access, flow and security. These were solved by giving the towers specific functions and linking the two towers used for the main vertical movement to the large multi-purpose area on the ground floor. In this way the various means of access from the street and underground car parks and the related security were made easily identifiable, centralized and integrated. Moreover, it meant access could be selected and oriented to the upper office quadrants and to facilities of more general interest and shared use, such as the library, conference rooms, exhibition space, press and printing department, etc.

The clarity and internal flexibility of this articulated structure means it will be able to respond to any complex future diversification requirements either of function or organization within the Bayer Group without upsetting the underlying architectural logic." (M. Bellini, from the Project Report).

Mario Bellini

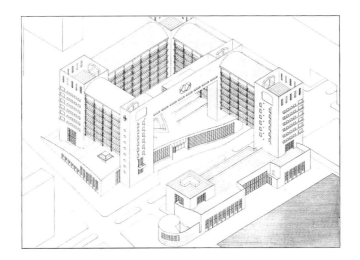

*Axonometric view from north of
phase A.
Site plan.*

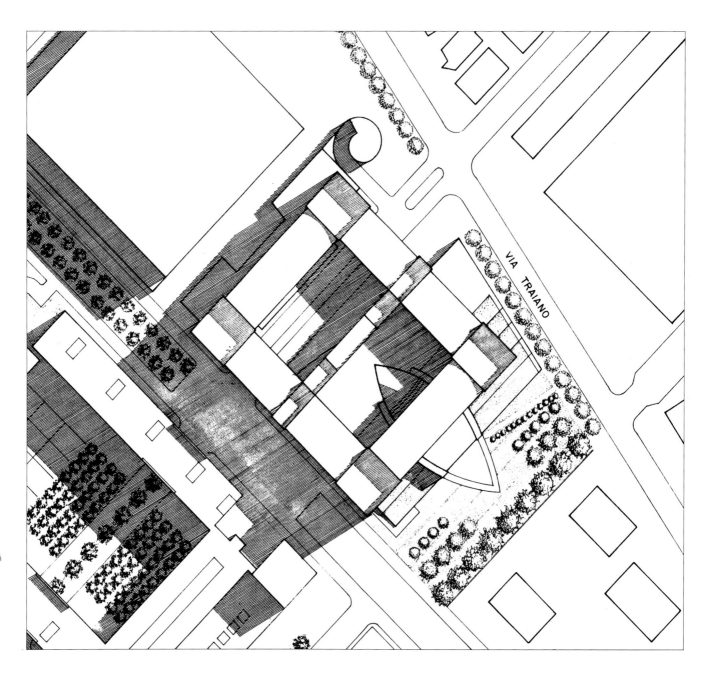

VIA TRAIANO

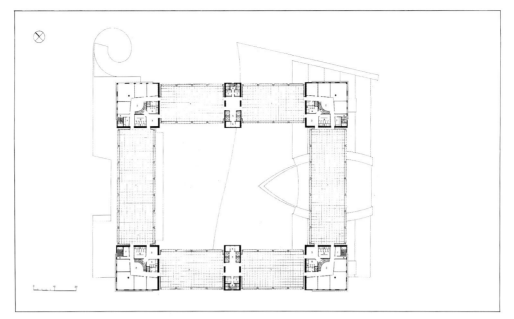

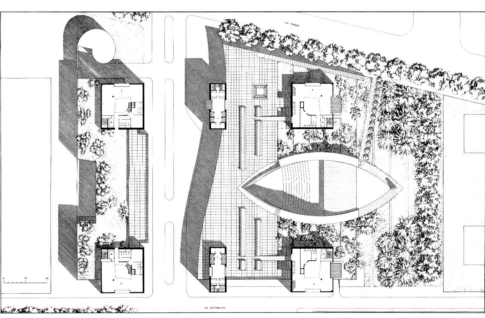

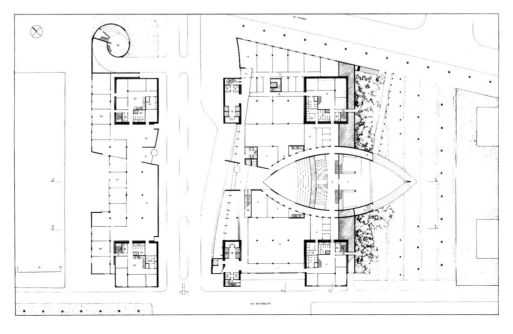

Elevation on the garden side.

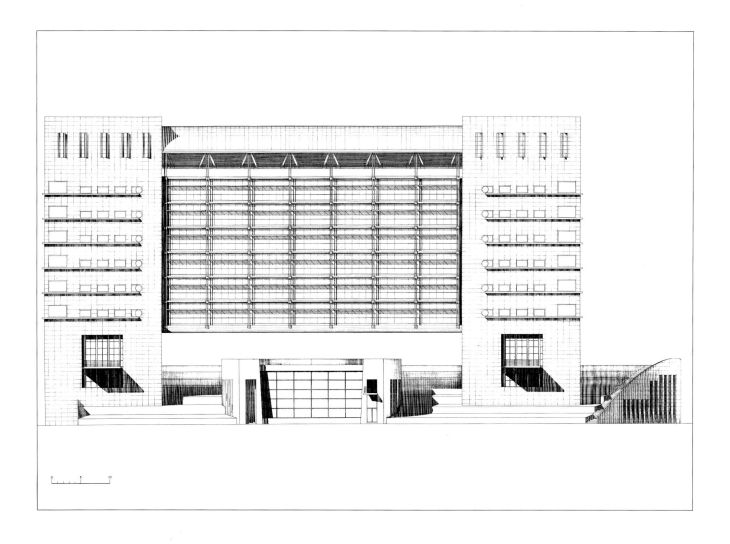

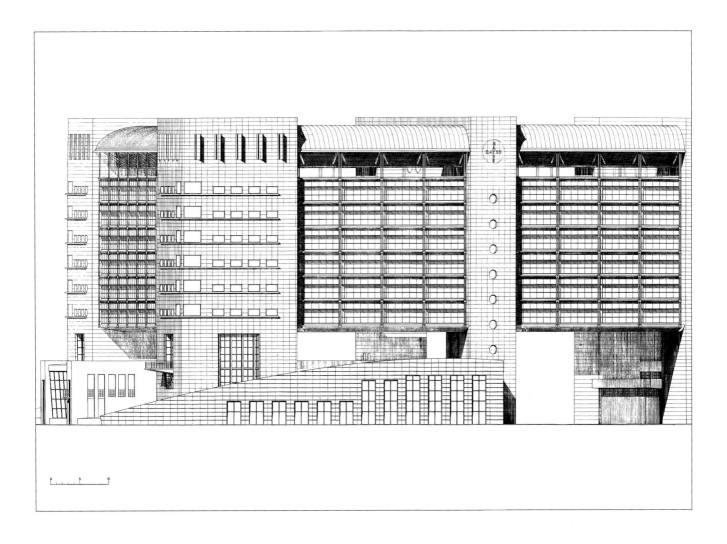

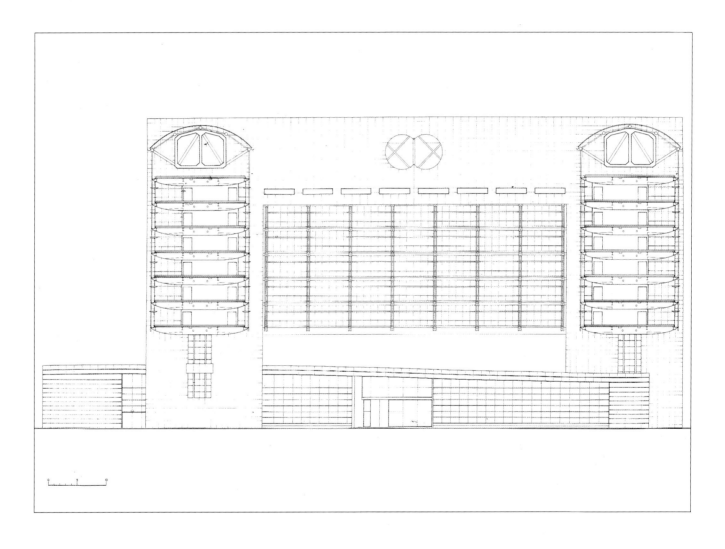

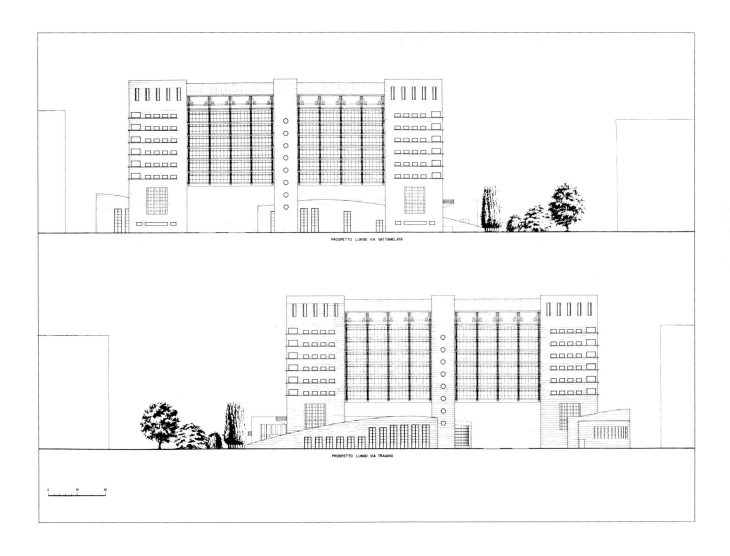

PROSPETTO LUNGO VIA GATTAMELATA

PROSPETTO LUNGO VIA TRAIANO

*Model view from Via Traiano and
interior details.*

Cassina Japan Showroom
Tokyo, Japan

location:
Minami Aoyama Collection
Building, Tokyo, Japan
client:
Cassina Japan Inc., Tokyo
project:
1989
executed:
1990

"Situated on the top floor of a new
building by Tadao Ando, the showroom is
organized round a double wall conceived
as a fragment of an aqueduct. This
characteristic element in the project
creates a relationship between the two
exhibition spaces: a large single space
bound by two glass and two cement walls
and an area with a low ceiling opening
onto a terrace." (M. Bellini, from the
Project Report).

Mario Bellini

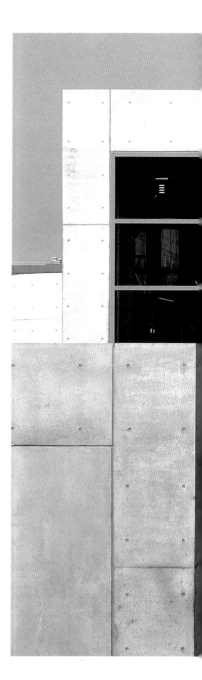

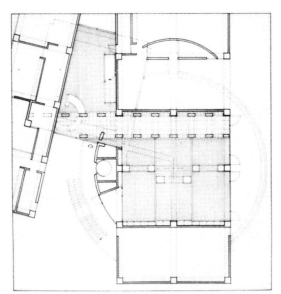
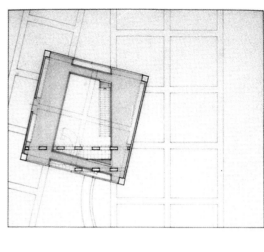

Interior and large multi-storey
atrium.

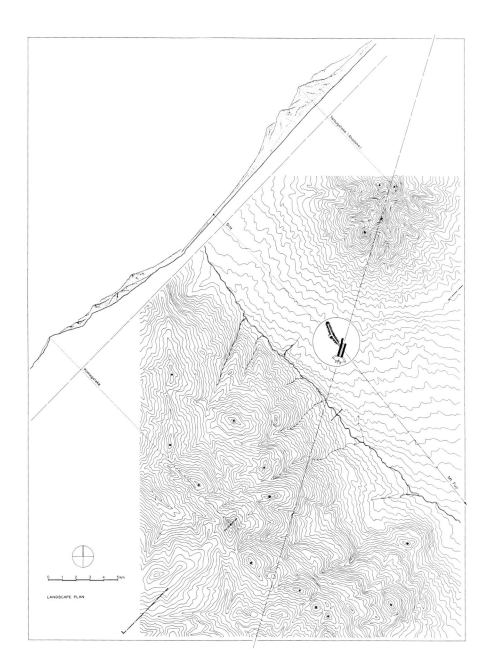

Diagram of the surrounding area.

Site plan.

Aerial view of the project.

LANDSCAPE PLAN

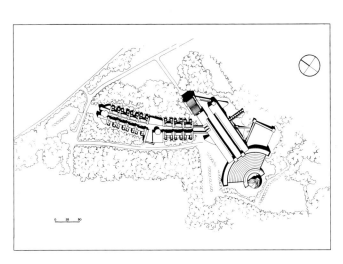

*Elevation on the internal street.
Plan of the internal street and the
apartments in a typical floor.*

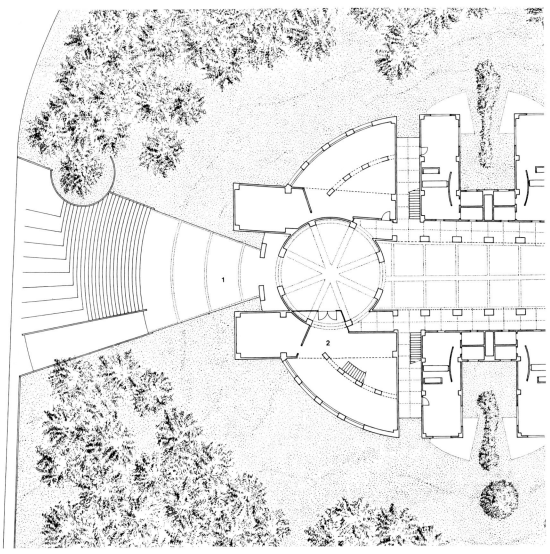

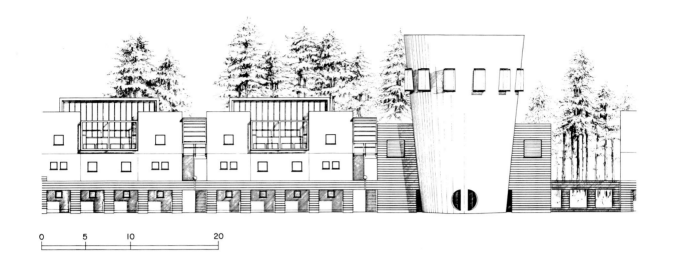

0 5 10 20

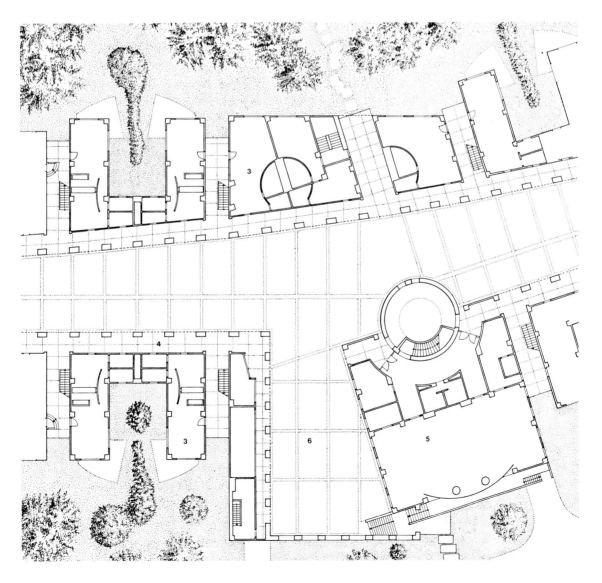

View of the internal street for the apartments.

Plans and cross section of the hotel.

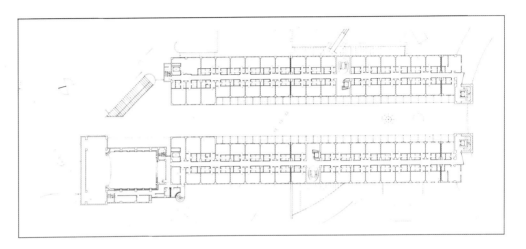

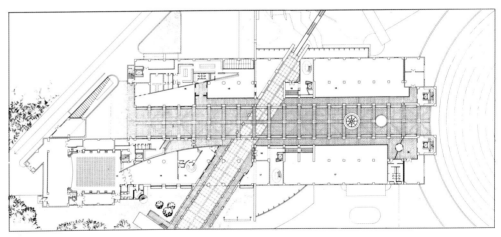

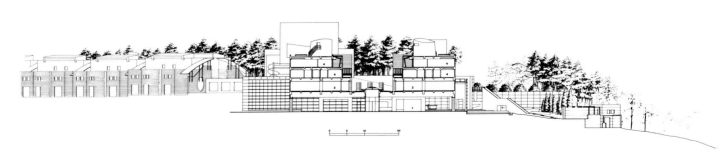

View of the hotel exterior.

Views of the auditorium.　　Longitudinal sections through the
hotel and auditorium.

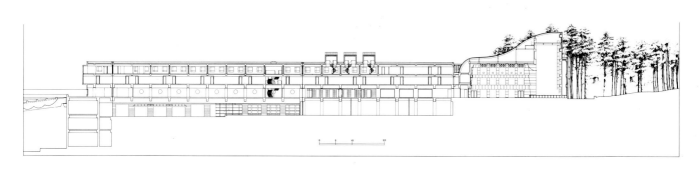

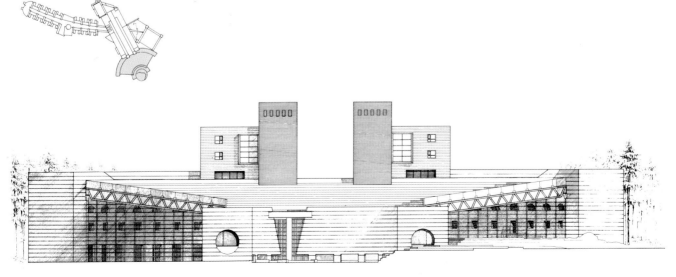

Swimming pool.

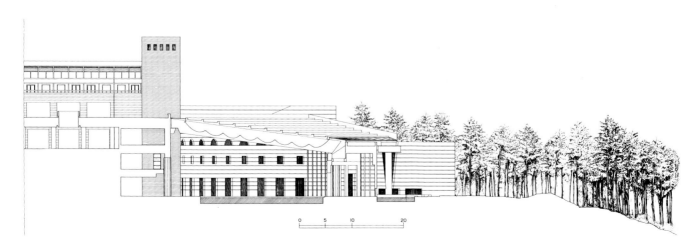

*Views of the indoor
swimming-pool.*

External view of the swimming pool.

Invited Consultation for "Berlin Morgen: Ideen für das Herz einer Großstadt"
Berlin, Germany

location:
Berlin, Germany
organizers:
Deutsches Architektur Museum
in conjunction with the *Frankfurter Allgemeine Zeitung*
project:
1990

"The notorious Wall has now gone. Broken into pieces and wrapped up like multicoloured chips, it is being sold off to tourists along with hot dogs round the Brandenburger Tor. Its evil is thus exorcised through an unconscious cannibalisation or fetishist sublimation (the largest pieces are mounted on stands and sold with a certificate of authenticity). But the traces of the former barrier have never been so conspicuous. Clumsy scars, they deface two hearts, two circulation systems, two heads and two contrasting life styles.

After the war the western half had to turn back on itself, invent a new center of gravity, new landmarks, new equilibria, because it was severed from those areas traditionally considered the city center. In the eastern half, on the other hand, the central areas were unnaturally pushed to the sidelines. They lost importance and status, because they had been unbalanced, cut off by the Wall. Then to add insult to injury they underwent the 'modernization' of buildings and road systems following the albeit praiseworthy reparation involving the complete reconstruction of the principal monuments destroyed by the war.

In such circumstances and given the very recent nature of the consultation, we can only but fully agree with the promoters' brief: the reunification of the city of Berlin raises many problems, but the true great theme is re-integrating the two centers of gravity, the reviving of a great multiple heart, organized in an organism that has been restored to unity and must now seek an identity, since it will never be the same as it was fifty years ago.

Kurfürstendamm, Gedächtniskirche, the Kulturforum, the Philharmonie, the Neue Nationalgalerie, the Hansa Viertel, the IBA, Kreuzberg, but even Fernsehturm and Karl Marx Allee all have their own contributions to make and must be taken into account when working out a new equilibrium. One thing is sure, however. The straightforward restoration of the pre-war status quo is not only physically out, but also culturally out.

Project Notes
Our proposal is organized at several levels of scale and depth. Two freeways must be introduced to the north of the Spree and the south of the Landwehrkanal (linking up with the large urban motorway system) to avoid through traffic from the west across and along the Tiergarten, the Museumsinsel and the mediaeval quarter. Fast traffic will be discouraged in these areas so as to rectify the post-war demolitions. These areas may be reached by a ring route and will be served by a system of underground car parks.
The areas to the southeast of the

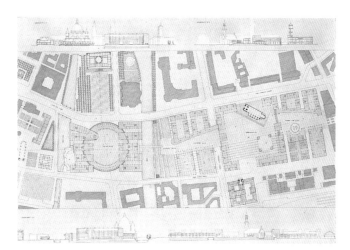

Tiergarten are still to be developed as transition zones between the park and the denser urban fabric of the city. They will be used for cultural-institutional purposes in line with a now familiar feature of the new Berlin.

Pariser Platz, Leipziger Platz and the Mehringplatz will be reunited, while the work of sewing up the blocks of Friedrichstadt will continue, and the demolished areas of Leipziger Strasse are to be re-integrated.

The redevelopment of Museumsinsel

Entirely given over to cultural and scientific institutions, the old Cölln will be transformed into a kind of floating Acropolis connected to the Unter den Linden and medieval Berlin by a huge complex dedicated to the Arts and Sciences and open to the public for a great variety of uses.

Standing along two branches of the Spree, the Museumsinsel will serve as a backdrop to the monumental historical avenue, just as the old Palace once did. The complex, however, will have a new typology as a more open central square organized transversally like a hinge opposite the Altes Museum.

The redevelopment of the medieval citadel

In the area between the Spree and the S-Bahn, inner-city railway tracks, this center will re-acquire a recognizable character along the lines of the pre-war layout. This will encourage its development as a high-density multifunctional services village bustling with life throughout the whole day.

Between the 'New Palace' and Alexanderplatz, in the re-integrated central sequence of blocks, an uninterrupted system of raised pedestrian precincts will be opened. These will be linked by a gallery to a central arcaded *Platz* facing towards the Marienkirche and the Rathaus and indirectly towards the 'New Palace' and the conserved Fernsehturm.

Rich with opportunities, places and levels, this *Platz* will be the symbol of the whole district and, beyond the fine backdrop created by the raised station, its bridgehead will be Alexanderplatz."

(M. Bellini, from the Project Report).

Mario Bellini

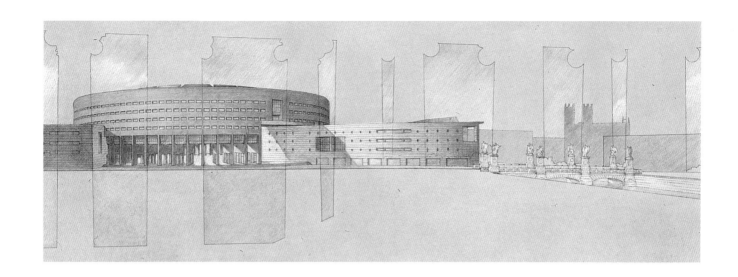

The new building seen from the
Altes Museum.

View of the square.

**Studio for Mario Bellini Associati Srl
Milan, Italy**

location:
Piazza Arcole 4, Milan, Italy
client:
Mario Bellini Associati Srl
project:
1990-93
executed:
1991-93

Mario Bellini designed his own studio in an old industrial building in Milan. The theme is now fairly familiar in Italian building practice: an old construction whose external parameters can't be touched must be redesigned by working on the internal space. Having accepted this constraint, the Milanese architect set about producing a twofold design: the conserved external walls are commented by inserting small features which successfully transform the existing structure; and the internal space is modelled very freely but without the pre-existing nature of the space being violated.

The design of the frames and casings, the small pergola round the courtyard highlighting the entrances and a large tree at the center of the space elegantly redeem the original industrial character of the building.

The heart of the internal space is a hall cutting across the whole building and marked off by metal columns and *ballatoi* (typical Milanese gallery-corridors). Culminating in a 'metaphysical' skylight, the hall provides access to all the work areas either by stairs or the lift situated on one side at the back of the hall.

But the most delightful surprises are encountered in exploring the studio, where a host of details indicate the 'semantic' wealth of this architecture. The door, subtly conjugated in all possible modes (sliding or folding doors, cornices, double cornices); the careful use of shutters to differentiate the connections between the various materials; and the plaster and exposed concrete connoting the varied character of the different places in the building.

Ermanno Ranzani

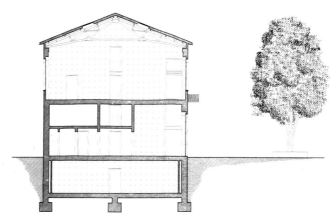

Cross section AA.

The project was for the whole courtyard; in part of it a space was created (marked blue) for the architect's own studio.

Mario Bellini Associati Studio: ground floor, mezzanine level, and first floor plans.

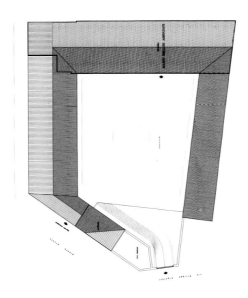

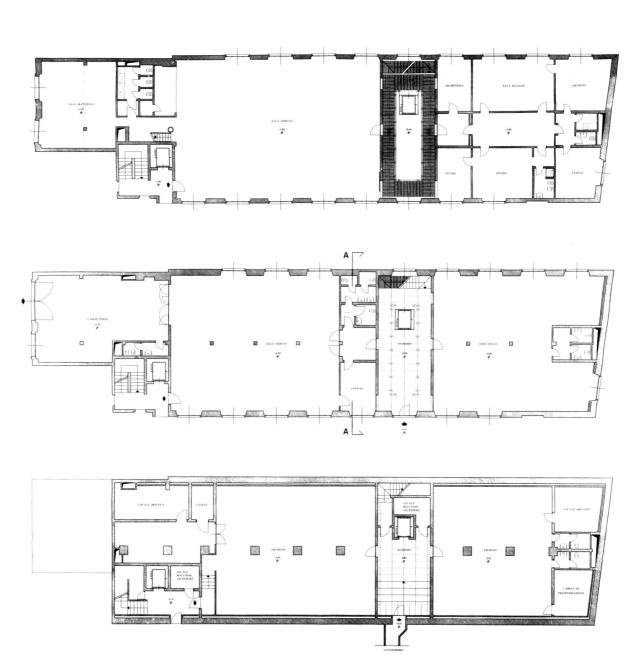

Courtyard.
The hall at ground level.

The hall at mezzanine level and on the first floor.

The work area.

The model workshop.

205

**Invited Consultation for the San
Donato Milanese Town Center
San Donato Milanese (Milan), Italy**

location:
San Donato Milanese (Milan), Italy
client:
SNAM SpA in conjunction with
the Comune di San Donato
Milanese
project:
1991

"This remarkable ten-hectare rectangle of open land right in the middle of San Donato provides an extraordinary opportunity to create a new town center. An incomplete perimeter with Propilei ('Propyleae') and an intersecting Gallery delimit the two main focal points of the town center – the Gardens and the Piazza del Mercato (marketplace) – joining and separating them from the surrounding urban fabric.

A large wooded green sloping 'terraced' space highlights the most important town buildings – the Theatre and Library/Picture Gallery – forming a kind of ideal Acropolis-Capitol. In the opposite direction the terraces bank down into the waters of the Bacino di San Donato.

A flat triangular area, the Largo del Municipio, links up the access steps to the Gardens, the Riva dei Giardini walkway and the Bacino with the major points of interest in the town: the Town Hall, Via M. di Cefalonia, Via Libertà, the Church and Via Emilia. A transverse passage across the Gardens joins them to the Via Iannozzi quarters, while a large arcaded street running lengthwise is flanked by a shopping gallery and links up with the Piazza della Chiesa, the small lake, the Cascina Roma-Church of San Donato area and the Via Libertà commercial quarter. The two axes meet in Piazzetta dei Giardini, which is extended by a covered way through the

Passaggio degli Affari, before intersecting with the Galleria delle Comunicazioni and coming out into the open again at the Rotonda degli Affari. The Gallery closes the Gardens to the south, and joining them up with the large Piazza del Mercato connects the Propilei Occidentali (Western Propyleae) with the Guardia Medica, the Theatre and the Passaggio del Commercio, while the Rotonda degli Affari is connected with the Library-Picture Gallery, the Sports Center and the Propilei Orientali (Eastern Propyleae).

The Piazza del Mercato to the south of the Gardens is at a tangent to the Galleria and is bound on three sides by the Propyleae. It also joins up with Via Gramsci through arcaded passages and with the southern quarters by three tree-lined streets. A large building with services structures follows the alignment of the Theatre and the Library-Picture Gallery, closing off the Rotonda degli Affari and extending on the external side in a large convex form. The Piazza del Mercato continues the custom of the weekly market held along Via Gramsci. All relatively low-slung with a regular compact outline, the propyleae lend a distinctive character to the area. They are mainly made up of a large passing arcade surmounted by three floors of housing."
(M. Bellini, from the Project Report).

Mario Bellini

*Typical cross section and external
courtyard facade.*

*Photomontage of the project in
context.*

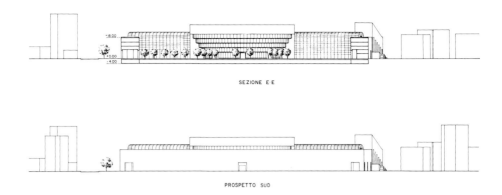

SEZIONE E E

PROSPETTO SUD

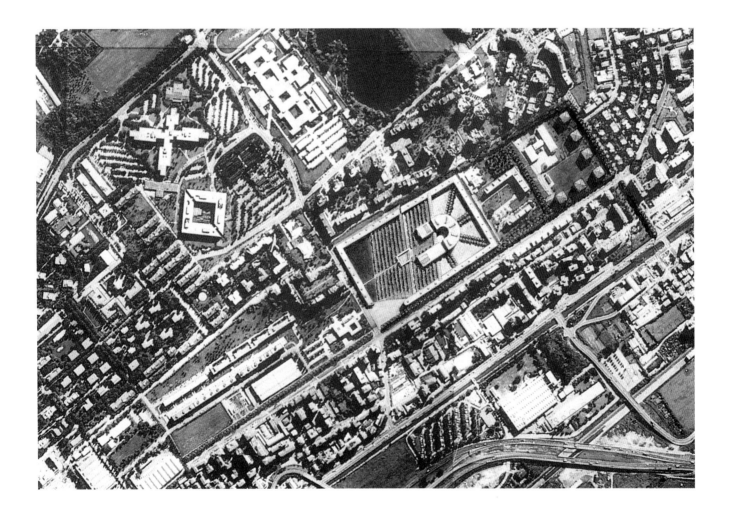

Site plan with elevations and sections.

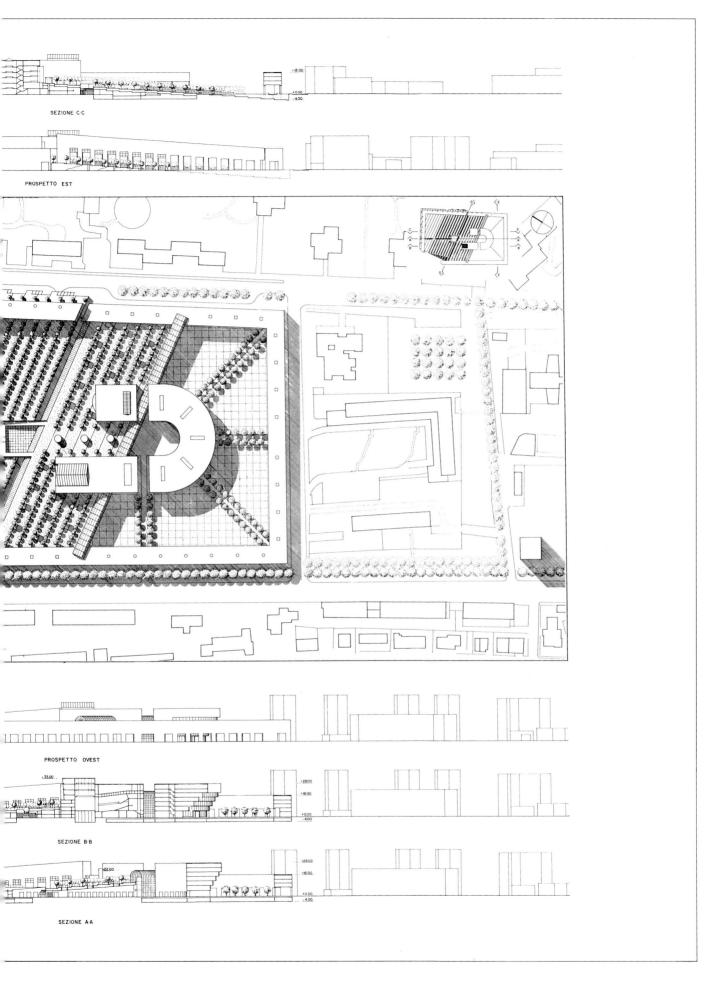

SEZIONE C-C

PROSPETTO EST

PROSPETTO OVEST

SEZIONE B-B

SEZIONE A-A

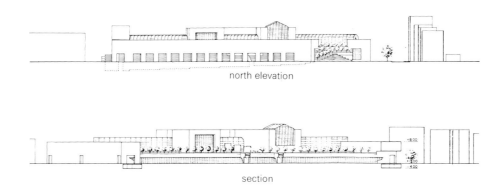

north elevation

section

Model views; elevation and section.

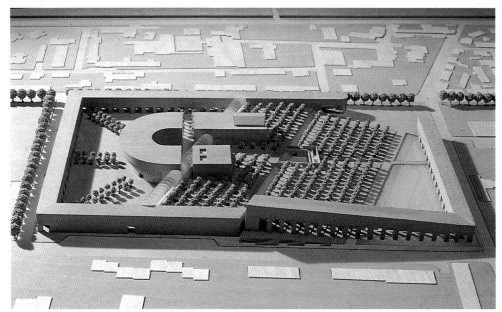

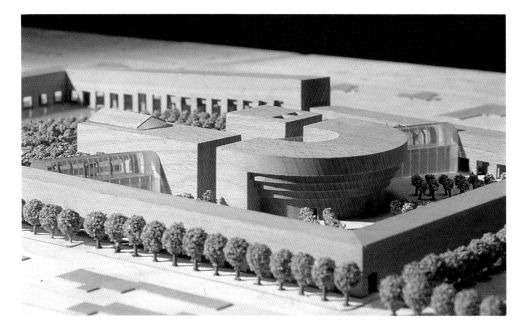

Ideas Competition for a Business Center in the Garibaldi-Repubblica Area, Milan, Italy

location:
the Garibaldi-Repubblica area,
Milan, Italy
competition organizer:
Comune di Milano-Associazione
degli Interessi Metropolitani (AIM)
project:
1991

"A disused railway area near the edge of the historic city, but also the center of an invisible web of transport systems, has been earmarked for a Business Center for over fifty years now. But this is primarily a piece of lip-service to the organicist metaphor of a city with all its arteries, heart, lungs and a head (namely, the business center). As a theme it fails to invite lasting testimonies – universal collective themes such as the cathedral, theatre and stadium.

Rather than an ephemeral Business Center what attracted us in the area was its center. The underlying tension of the empty urban space seemed to be crying out for an important theme able to give a meaning to such mindless places. We were also struck by the fact that five important roads converge on the same center.

Here we introduced the classical sequence of the *Rondò* (large inner-city roundabout) with the counterpoint of a tree-lined promenade: this magnificent sequence is well-established in European cities: the *rond-point* of the Etoile and the Champs-Elysées in Paris, or the Place Wilson and the *grandes allées* in Dijon. It is a significant collective theme enhancing and celebrating the city for centuries to come, because it builds into its memory the promise of long life.

The heart of the *Rondò* is basically a circular piazza – like the Place des Victoires or the Belle-Alliance Platz. For centuries such structures have been considered more beautiful when the geometric rigour of the plan is matched with identical facades or at least with equal elements. In this case we decided that the inner circular arcade should have a uniform architecture.

The *Rondò* consists of a central drum containing the slip roads and the Piazza and Towers. The tree-lined promenade stretches away from base. Except for a double continuous row on the southern edge, the promenade has been planted with square garden courts delimited on the north edge by a light portico.

The Piazza and its Towers and Promenade are the main themes of the project. Although undeniably new and almost futuristic (a circular junction with a halo of skyscrapers), the project is also solidly ancient, an instantly recognizable combination of two well-known urban figures almost naturally set in a monumental landscape. And this will be so even in centuries to come when traffic jams will no longer be remembered, just as we have lost the memory of the rumbling carriages blocking up the *faubourgs* in the eighteenth-century or Broadway in the nineteenth century." (M. Bellini, M. Romano, from the Project Report).

Mario Bellini and *Marco Romano*

Site plan and model view.

following pages
*Perspective view of the large
central space.*

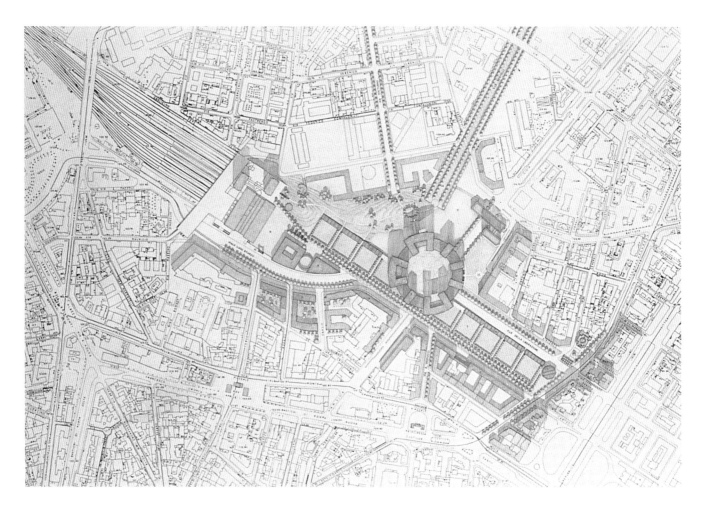

The inner area of the square.

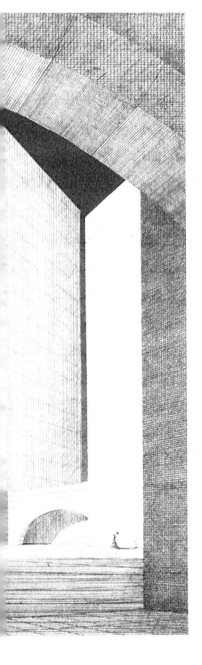

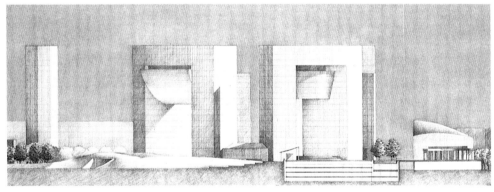

Primary School
Giussano (Milan), Italy

location:
Via Massimo d'Azeglio, Giussano
(Milan), Italy
client:
Comune di Giussano
project:
1991
executed:
1992-95

"The building is situated at the corner of Via Massimo d'Azeglio with a newly constructed street intended to provided more protected pedestrian access to the school and create a single large green space between the existing public buildings and the new school.

The school is composed of two parts clearly differentiated in architectural terms:

1) The classroom block is closely linked to the green area with sunlit conditions and pleasant views as a backdrop to school activities.

2) The blocks containing the lecture hall, gymnasium and dining-room are directly linked to the surrounding urban context and attached to the single-space cylindrical volume of the entrance hall – the focal point for all the other parts of the building.

The architectural element connecting the parts is a double undulating lamellar wood beam. Starting outside as the support for the large entrance canopy, the beam crosses the hall and then drops down to link up the classroom block.

The choice of material reflected the various architectural meanings of the school's constituent parts:

1) The classroom block. To provide the greatest transparency with the green area, fully glazed walls are used. The doors and window frames are made of painted aluminium, the roofs are wood with copper finishing, while the walls between classes are plastered and the floors made of wood.

The use of wood makes the classrooms and teaching areas warm and almost homely.

2) The Gymnasium, Lecture Hall, Refectory and Entrance Hall. These compact solid structures with few openings towards the street, designed to protect the school environment, are made of reinforced concrete finished with plaster and horizontal strips of grey stone.

3) The Main Hall. The ground-floor lower section is glazed towards the entrance and the internal area of the gardens and classrooms. The compact cylindrical first floor has slit windows and is made of exposed reinforced concrete with horizontal lines of 'shutters'. The central skylight has a glazed perimeter, wood covering and copper external finishing." (from the Project Report).

Design sketches.

Overall model view.

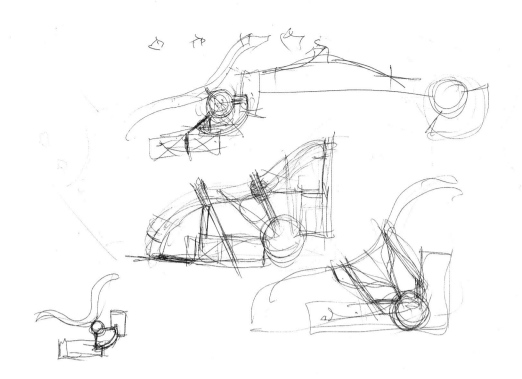

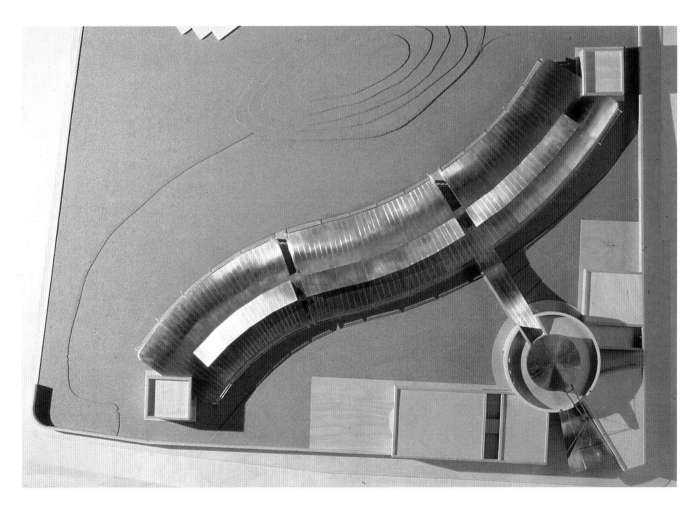

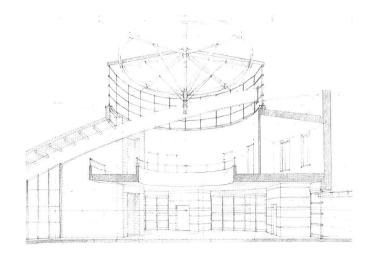

Ground floor plan.
1. Entrance area.
2. Classrooms and corridor.
3. Services.

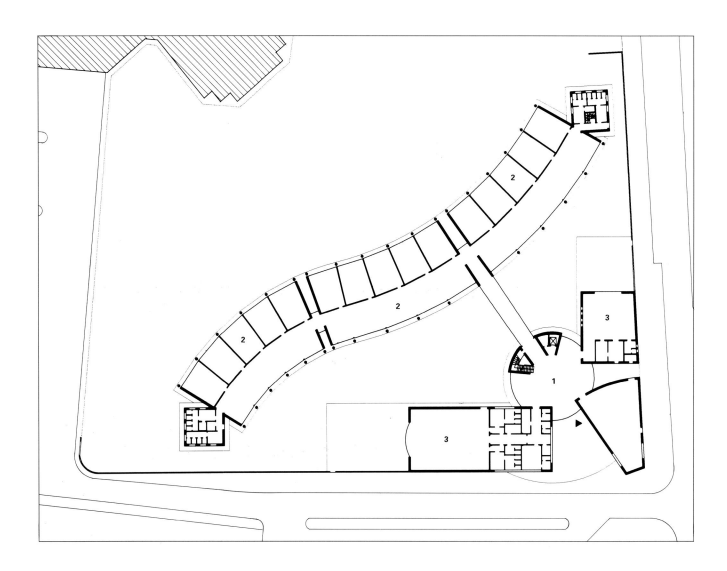

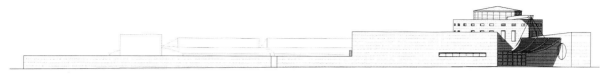

north elevation

west elevation

south courtyard elevation

south classroom elevation

north classroom elevation

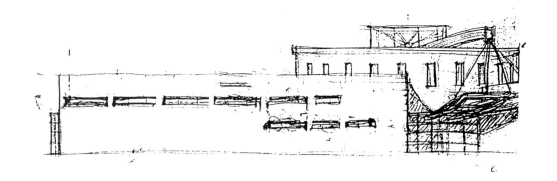

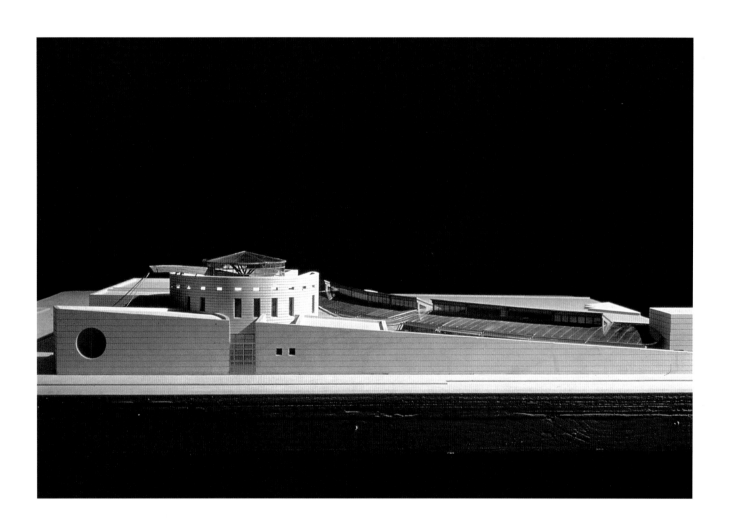

Design sketches.

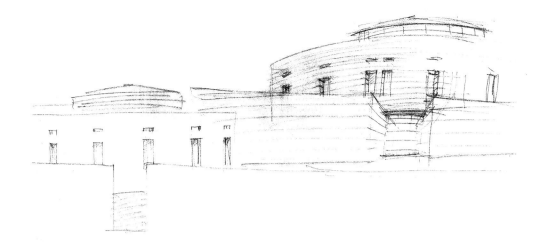

Model views.

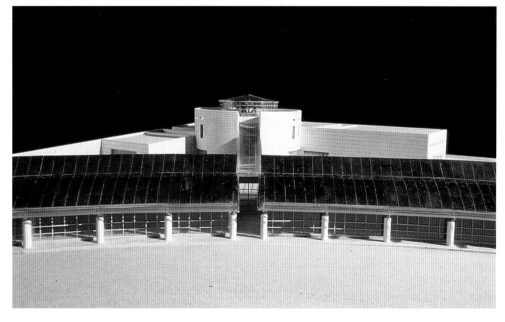

Model and building construction.

**Design for the Goshikidai Marine
Resort Complex
Kagawa-Ken, Japan**

location:
Goshikidai, Kagawa-ken, Japan
client:
Nichii Co., Ltd., Osaka
project:
1992-93

The redevelopment of a former salt-works provided the opportunity to create a large holiday resort near the sea.

The functional elements are a small port, large hotel and holiday residences distributed in a park created out of the salt-pan itself.

The main design aim is to use the theme of the small port and the hotel in one very powerful architectural idea as the fulcrum for the organization of the open space. The residences are arranged in small groups around this fulcrum. The relation between the exceptional and the normal is established by the varied architectural treatment of the parts of the project.

A large arcaded courtyard towards the sea, with at its head a tall, highly plastic metallic building, orders the space; large pergolas contain the residences thus giving different cuts to units with the same general plan.

A number of Bellini's favourite themes reappear in this project. They are to be found in the 'metaphysical' aura of the large arcades of the marina; the 'constructionist' sense in the plans of the overall organization of the spaces and the great care over designing the green areas.

Ermanno Ranzani

General organisation of project.
Site plan and section.

Model view.

Site plan.

Plan and elevations of the hotel
and harbour.

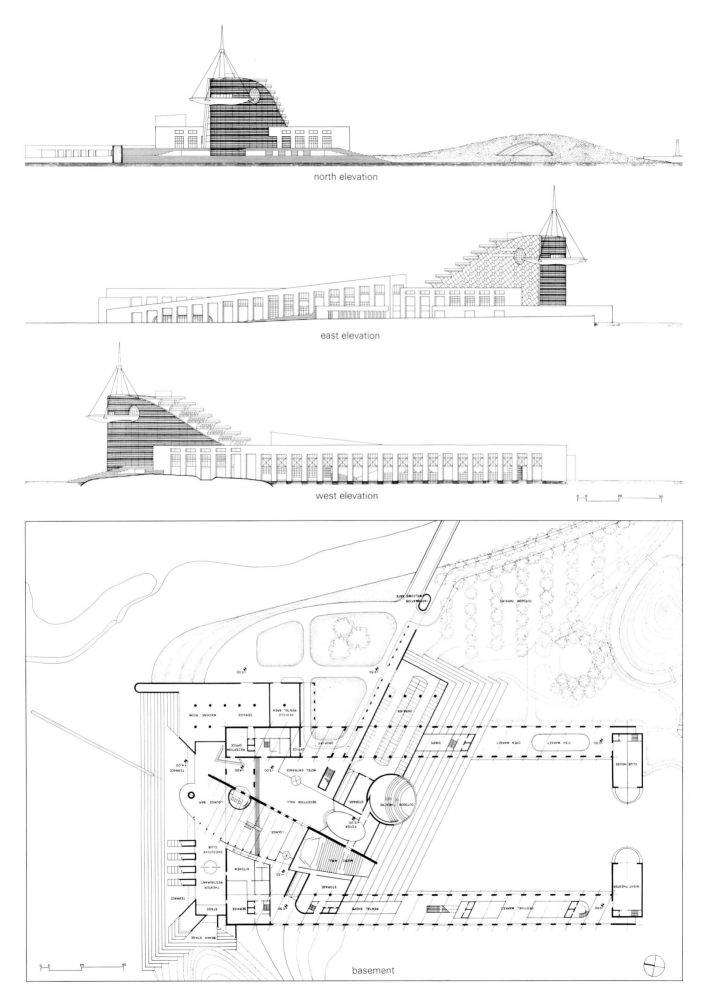

north elevation

east elevation

west elevation

0 5   25   50

basement

0 2   25   50

229

The apartments; plan and sections.

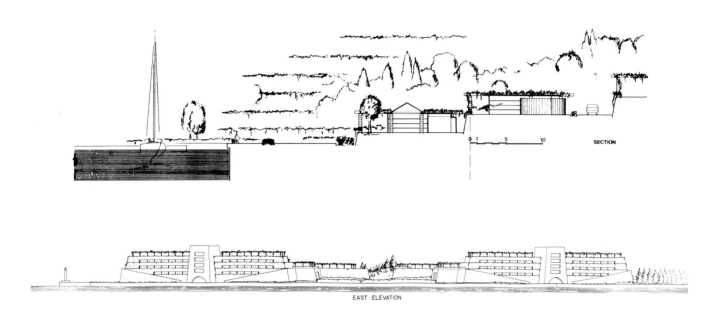

SECTION

EAST ELEVATION

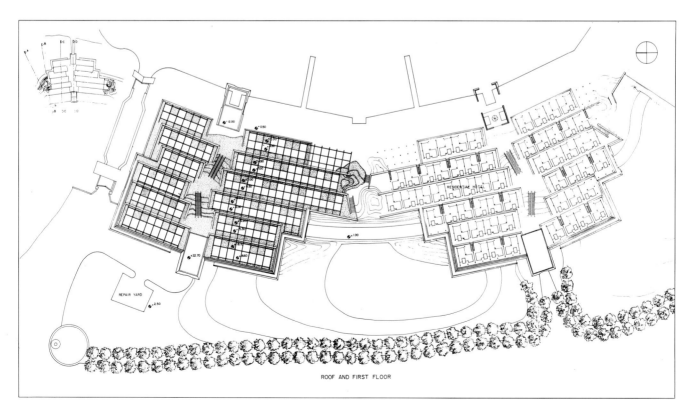

REPAIR YARD

RESIDENTIAL HOTEL

ROOF AND FIRST FLOOR

Model views.

location:
Beniyas Road, Dubai Creek New
Marina, Deira, Dubai, United Arab
Emirates
client:
Al-Rostamani Group
of Companies, Dubai
project:
1994

"Situated on a privileged site, the corner between the waterfront and a square, the lot was created in the context of the new city council plan for the area along the creek cutting through the heart of Dubai. Set on a two-storey base (a shopping Mall), an apartment tower soars up, sculpted like a great half-wave leaping from the second to the twenty-third floor beyond the arcaded enclosure round the square. To the west, a convex surface ends in a cascade of balconies, and to the east in a cylindrical tower indicating the entrances and supporting a circular swimming-pool, spectacularly set overhanging the city. A twenty-one storey prism – the Office Block – closes off the wave-shaped building and bounds a tapering single-space glass hall."
(M. Bellini, from the Project Report).

Mario Bellini

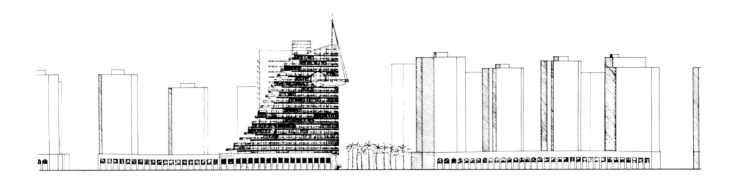

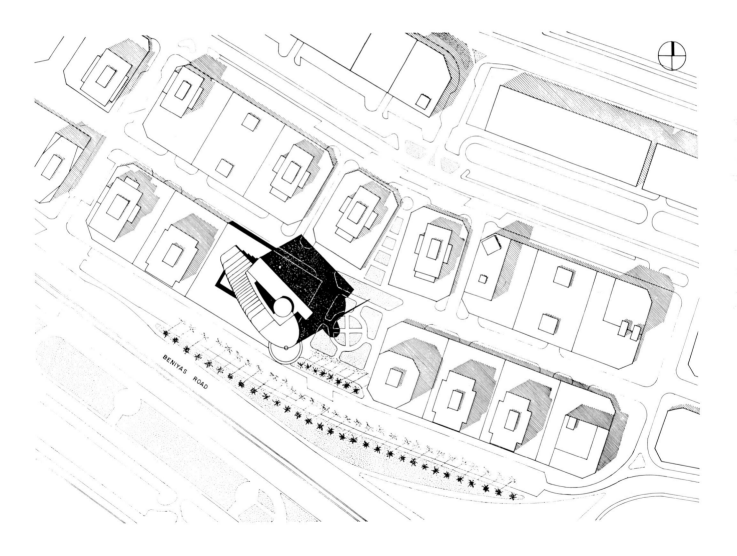

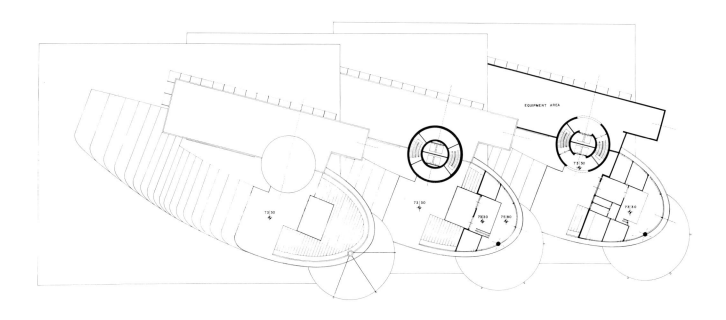

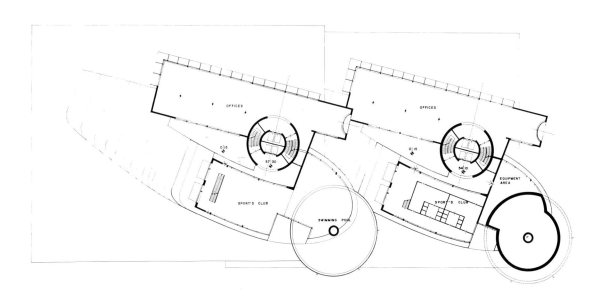

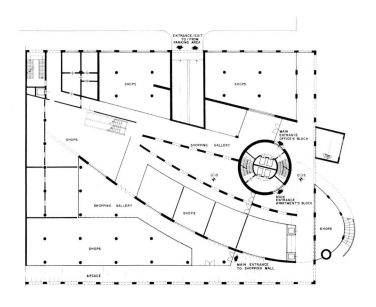

236

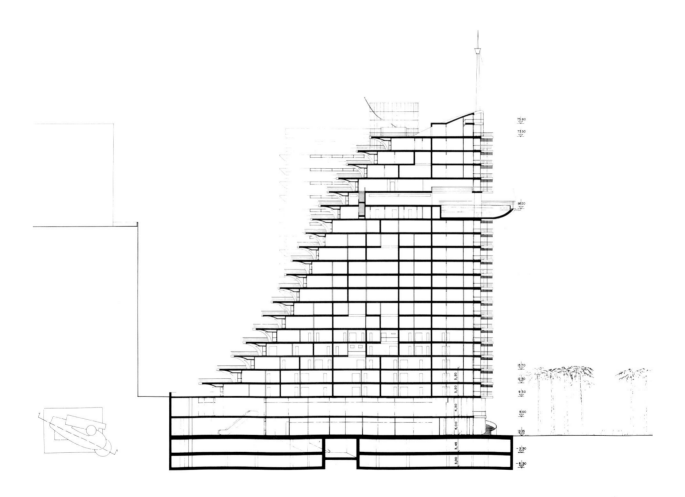

239

Elevations and model views.

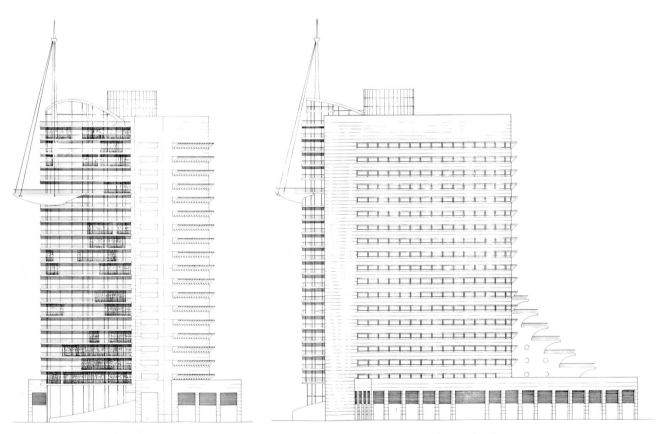

south-east elevation   north-east elevation

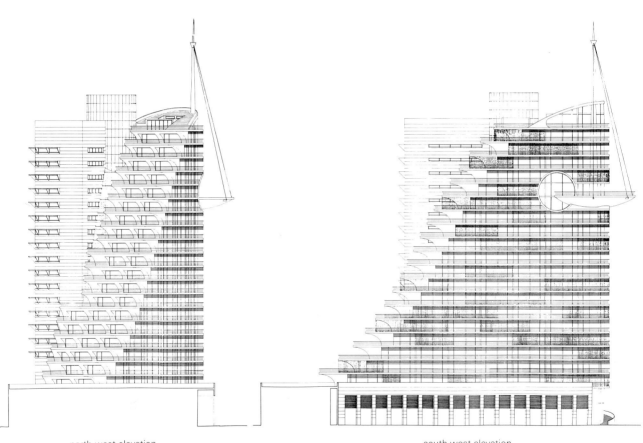

north-west elevation   south-west elevation

1994-ongoing

New branch for the Schmidtbank and redevelopment of the surrounding area with the creation of a new square, Limbach-Oberfrohna, Germany

location:
Albert Einstein Strasse-
Johannisplatz,
Limbach-Oberfrohna, Germany
client:
Schmidtbank-Zentrale Hof,
Germany
project:
1994
executed:
ongoing

"The architectural choices for this project closely follow the context. Firstly, a new tree-lined square is planned on the Külz Strasse. This will benefit both from the shopping facilities in the street and the re-opening of a new museum in a space created out of an existing construction. The real building work, however, concerns a construction with a triangular plan housing the services of the new Schmidtbank branch.
The building consists of two parts with different functions: the reserved areas of the bank and the more public counter areas.
The architecture emphasizes this organization enabling the building to order the neighbouring urban spaces: the roadside facade is built in bricks and concrete (just as the surrounding buildings are); while the front on the square is fully glazed, creating a strong sense of continuity between inside and out." (from the Project Report).

LIMBACH OBER FROHNA
27 DIC '93

Site plan.

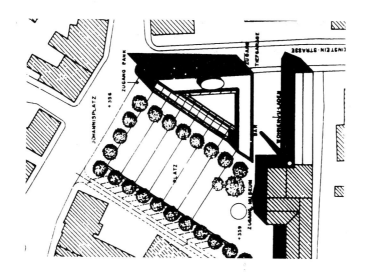

Ground floor plan.

Typical office floor plan.

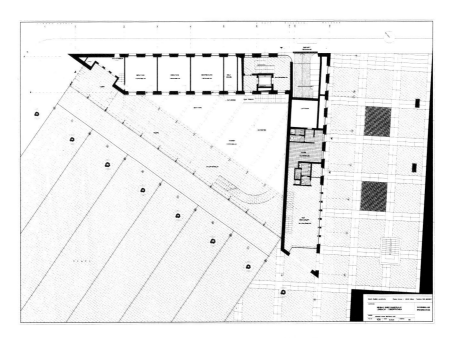

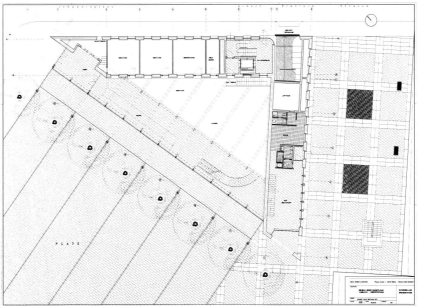

Elevations.

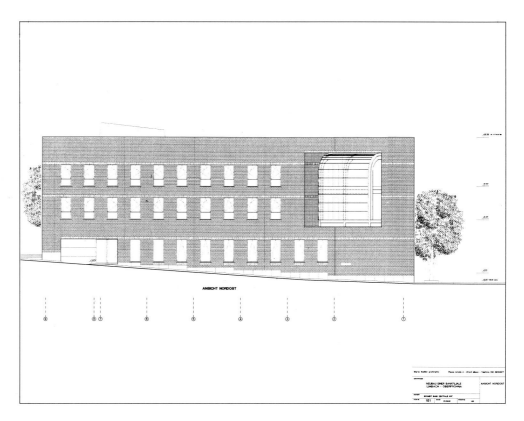

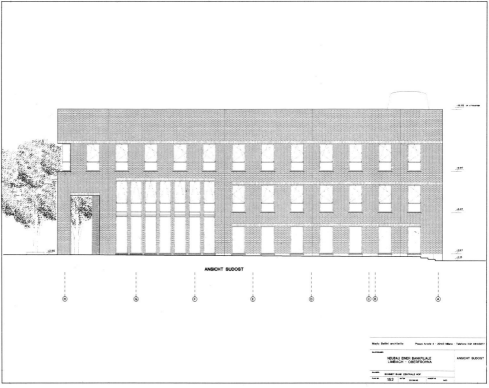

Cross sections.

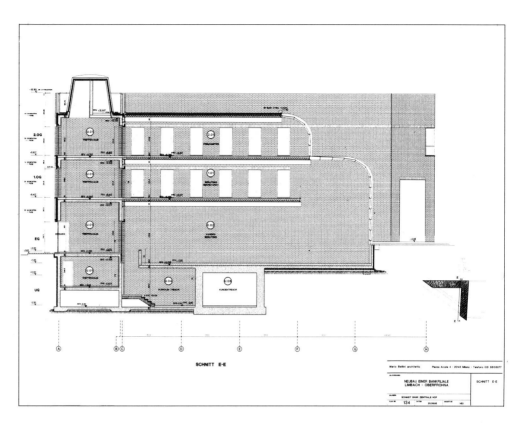

SCHNITT E-E

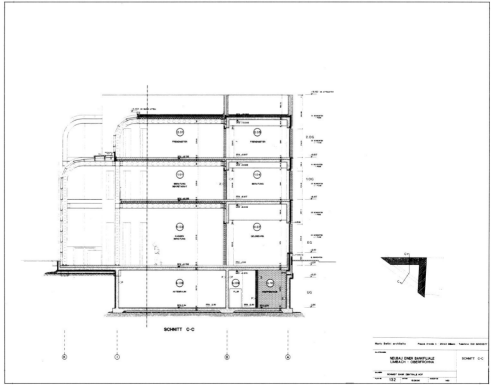

SCHNITT C-C

Model views.

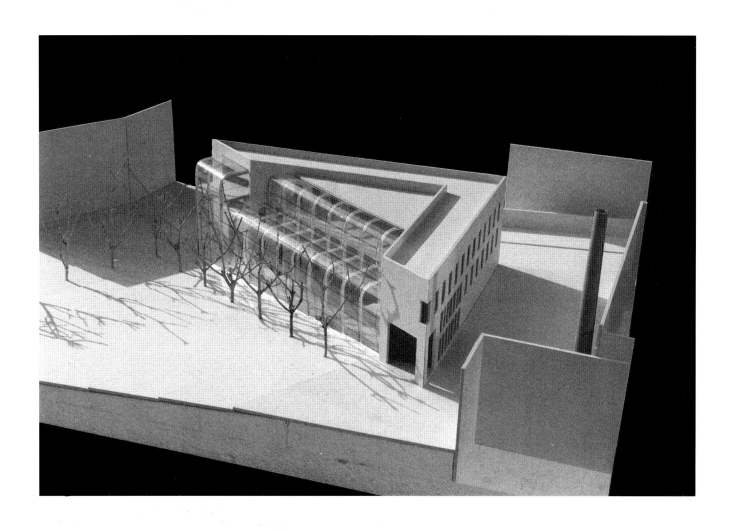

location:
Yokohama, Japan
competition organisers:
city of Yokohama, Japan
project:
1994

"A number of landmarks give the
Yokohama port its distinctive character:
the Bay Bridge, the Minato Mirai towers
and the Yamashita Park waterfront.
Given the constraints of the competition
brief and the planning functions required,
the terminal will have to face tough
competition from other elements in the
area. Moreover, it also seems difficult to
create a link between the terminal and the
city.
In view of this situation, our building
seeks to solve the problems by
emphasizing the force of the roof.

Like a great wave, it becomes a walkaway
rising from the city level up to thirty-one
metres.
An inviting double row of palms marks off
a walkway of five hundred metres
ascending from the road level to a
sightseeing rotunda overlooking the port.
A straight green boulevard cuts
diagonally across the port bay – an
instantly recognizable sight for anyone
arriving by sea."
(M. Bellini, from the Project Report).

Mario Bellini

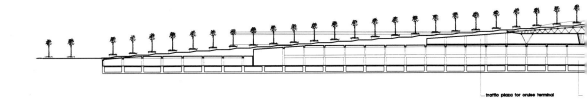

traffic plaza for cruise terminal

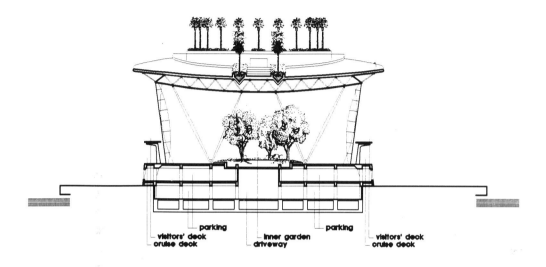

parking   parking
visitors' deck   inner garden   visitors' deck
cruise deck   driveway   cruise deck

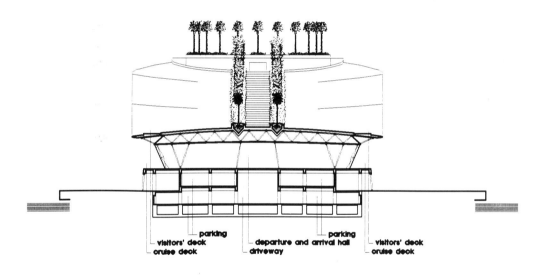

parking   parking
visitors' deck   departure and arrival hall   visitors' deck
cruise deck   driveway   cruise deck

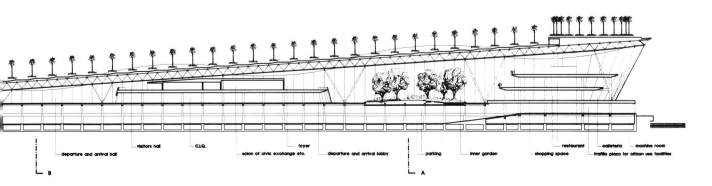

departure and arrival hall   visitors' hall   C.I.Q.   salon of civic exchange etc.   foyer   departure and arrival lobby   parking   inner garden   shopping space   restaurant   cafeteria   machine room   traffic plaza for citizen use facilities

B   A

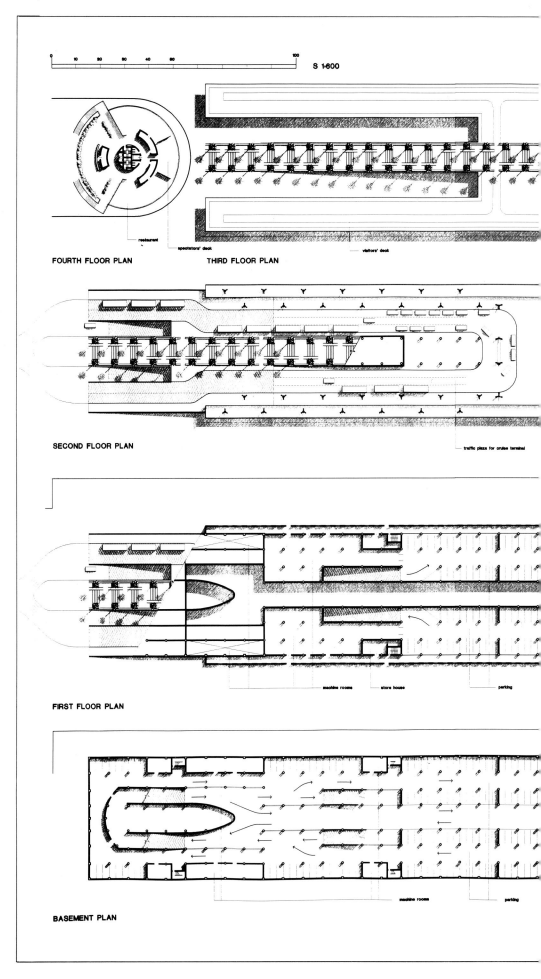

S 1:600

FOURTH FLOOR PLAN   THIRD FLOOR PLAN

restaurant

spectators' deck   visitors' deck

SECOND FLOOR PLAN

traffic plaza for cruise terminal

FIRST FLOOR PLAN

machine rooms   store house   parking

BASEMENT PLAN

machine rooms   parking

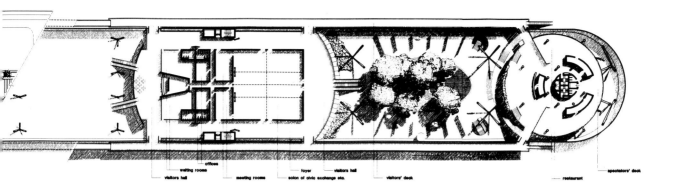

visitors hall   offices   meeting rooms   foyer   visitors hall   visitors' deck   restaurant   spectators' deck
waiting room   solon of civic exchange etc.

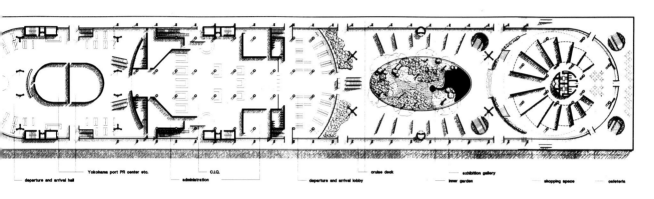

departure and arrival hall   Yokohama port PR center etc.   administration   C.I.Q.   departure and arrival lobby   cruise deck   exhibition gallery   inner garden   shopping space   cafeteria

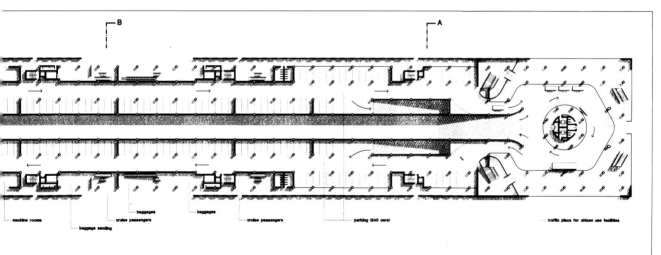

B   A

machine rooms   baggage   baggage   cruise passengers   parking (240 cars)   traffic plaza for citizen use facilities
baggage sending   cruise passengers

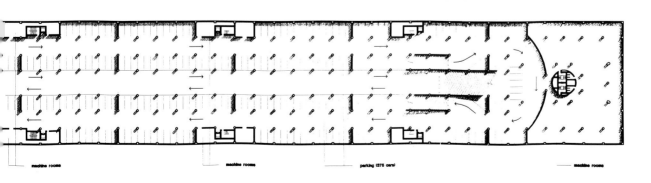

machine rooms   machine rooms   parking (375 cars)   machine rooms

*Computer graphic studies. The
project in context and views of the
interior.*

**Exhibition Designs for
"The Renaissance from Brunelleschi
to Michelangelo. The representation
of architecture"**

location:
Palazzo Grassi, Venice, Italy;
Musée National des Monuments
Français, Paris, France; Altes
Museum, Berlin, Germany
client:
Palazzo Grassi SpA, Venice;
Musée National des Monuments
Français, Paris; Kunstbibliothek,
Berlin
dates:
1994-95

"The exhibition brings together almost all surviving fifteenth and sixteenth century wooden architectural models, as well as numerous paintings, manuscripts and drawings by the greatest Renaissance architects, testifying to the complexity and cultural wealth of their age.

The itinerary enables visitors to explore the principal themes in depth. The main challenge in the project was how to present such a great variety of objects and historical evidence in meaningful theme groups following a sequence of such well-defined settings.

Moreover, we felt that special care needed to be taken in giving the whole exhibition design the right kind of distinctive 'atmosphere'.

The desired ambience – that sense of 'magical' suspension within the exhibition – was achieved by the careful use of light, also conceived in such a way as to meet the different requirements for each particular category of objects.

The 'theme' of the design thus became providing the right lighting for the various items: old drawings (light paper, monochromed, two dimensions, not more than 50 lux tolerated), Renaissance models (dark wood, large and three-dimensional, heavy resistance to light), painted canvases and boards (intense colours, very variable dimensions, medium resistance to light), objects,

low-reliefs and inlays. It could therefore be described as being substantially a 'light-oriented design'.

To avoid the diffusion of undesired light, all natural light sources were abolished, and all the walls of the rooms and new surfaces were painted medium-light opaque grey with a touch of purple to obtain a 'grey distance' effect.

The drawings were laid out on independent panels and individually illuminated by thin optical fibre sources. Resting on wall tables or on large free-standing display units (the tops covered with waxed black rolling-mill sheet-iron were supported by pine trestles), the models were lit by strong incident light so as to throw into relief the architectural chiaroscuro.

In some rooms an 'apparatus' was installed to 'stage-set' a particular theme. Thus, for example, in the room dedicated to Renaissance building-sites, a full-scale reconstruction was made of the scaffolding used for the restoration of the lantern of the cupola of Florence Cathedral, while for the room displaying the *Ideal City*, from Urbino, a 'perspective reaction' device was mounted. In this way the real dimension of the room was distorted to reveal the concept of 'contrived naturalness' underlying 'representation' as intended in the Renaissance.

Great care was also taken to characterize

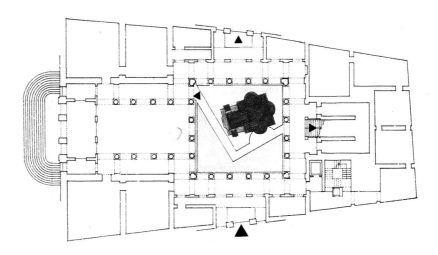

every room in the exhibition with prominent features creating a well-defined sequence of visual stages alternated with a complex system of additional material and cross-references displayed in each room binding the exhibition into an organic whole.

A decisive role was played by the graphic design in giving the whole exhibition conceptual unity: the subtle individually lit titles of the rooms, the extensive quotations from contemporary Renaissance texts, the many complex synoptic tables and the beautiful drawings enlarged for closer examination (all silkscreened on the grey 'distance' of the walls, in white, dark grey and only a few other colours). All of these elements played their part in linking up and enhancing the exhibition itinerary."
(M. Bellini, from the Project Report).

Mario Bellini

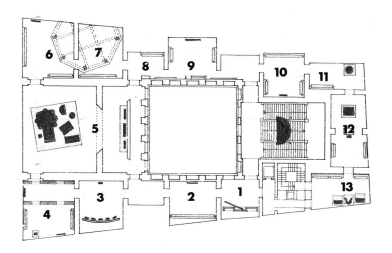

Plans of the first and second floor rooms; views of the rooms with Renaissance models.

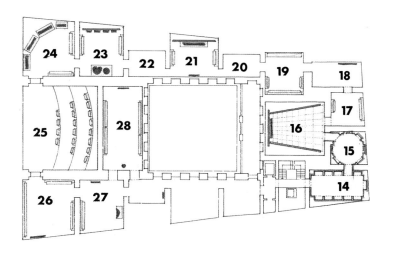

*Room with display cases and
diagram of the display-case
funcions.*

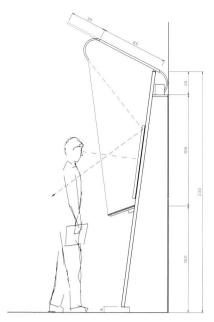

Reconstruction of the scaffolding
used in building Santa Maria del
Fiore.

following pages
The Palazzo Grassi stairway and
model of dome for St Peter's.

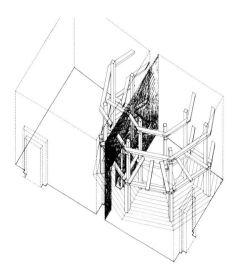

259

Project data

**Exhibition Designs
for "The Treasures
of San Marco"
1984-87**

exhibition Centers:
Grand Palais, Paris, France;
Römisch-Germanisches Museum,
Cologne, Germany; British
Museum, London, United
Kingdom; Metropolitan Museum
of Art, New York, USA; Los
Angeles County Museum of Art,
Los Angeles, USA; Dallas
Museum of Art, Dallas, USA; Art
Institute of Chicago, Chicago,
USA; Palazzo del Quirinale, Rome,
Italy; Palazzo Reale, Milan, Italy;
and Palazzo Ducale, Venice, Italy
client:
Ing. C. Olivetti & SC. Spa, Ivrea
(Turin), Italy; the exhibition was
organized by the Olivetti Cultural
Relations Board in conjunction
with the Procuratoria di San
Marco, Venice, la Réunion des
musées nationaux, Paris, and the
Metropolitan Museum of Art,
New York
dates:
1984-87
architect:
Mario Bellini, Mario Bellini
Associati Srl
design team:
G. Bonfanti
graphic design:
R. Pieraccini, Ing. C. Olivetti & C.
SpA
display design:
Mario Bellini in collaboration with
D. Bellini and G. Bonfanti
lighting:
Mario Bellini Associati Srl
principal materials:
painted plasterboard; display

case – stainless steel painted with
Nextel
selected bibliography:
Mario Bellini Architetture, Electa,
1988, pp. 22-23
Mario Bellini designer (edited by
C. McCarty), The Museum of
Modern Art, New York, 1987

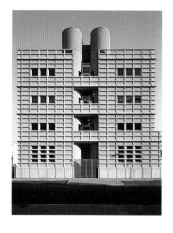

Offices and Industrial Complex
1984-88

location:
Via Kuliscioff, Milan, Italy
client:
Scotti Immobiliare SpA, Milan
project:
from 1984
executed:
1986-88
architect:
Mario Bellini, Mario Bellini Associati Srl
design team:
G. Origlia, C. Pedrazzini
collaborators:
O. De Luca, L. Morandi
project management:
C. Ferrari, Scotti Immobiliare SpA
structures:
G. Finazzi, Bergamo
installations:
Copresit Srl, Milan
quantity surveyors:
Mario Bellini Associati Srl, Scotti Immobiliare SpA
director of works:
Mario Bellini Associati Srl
artistic director:
Mario Bellini Associati Srl
contractors:
Cattaneo Costruzioni, Bergamo
site area:
25,000 m^2
floor area:
31,000 m^2
volume:
122,000 m^3
tender budget:
30 billion lira
purpose:
The two aligned buildings on Via Kuliscioff house spaces for service activities; the buildings to

the rear are for industrial use
office buildings structure:
in situ reinforced concrete (r.c.); the floor slabs over the arch hang from three large steel roof trusses
industrial buildings structure:
precast r.c.
principal materials:
the facades are made with precast r.c. and grit panels distinguished by their three-dimensional pattern and surface treatment; the perimeter ridges are smooth, whereas the internal sections are sandblasted to bring out the colour and grain of the marble used as aggregates. Designed on a 120 x 60 cm module, each panel stretches the height of an entire floor (360 x 240 cm).
selected bibliography:
Casabella, no. 557, May 1989, pp. 36-39
Mario Bellini Architetture, Electa, 1988, pp. 38-47
Milano. Architetture per la città. 1980-1990, Editoriale Domus, 1989, p. 130

Offices and Landscaping for the Cassano D'Adda Thermoelectric Power Station
1985-90

location:
Cassano d'Adda (Milan), Italy
client:
Azienda energetica municipale Milano (Aem)
project:
1985
executed:
1986-90
architect:
Mario Bellini, Mario Bellini Associati Srl
design team:
L. Morandi, G. Origlia, C. Pedrazzini
collaborators:
E. Gueli, P. Lissi, O. De Luca
model:
Mario Bellini Associati Srl
interior design:
G. Origlia, Milan
project management:
Lorenzetti (Aem)
structural engineer:
M. Locatelli, Milan
electrical installations:
ELC, Milan
quantity surveyors:
Cairoli (Aem)
director of works:
Mario Bellini Associati Srl
artistic director:
Mario Bellini Associati Srl
contractors:
CO.E.S.MI., Milan
site area:
210,000 m^2
floor area:
3,310 m^2

volume:
9,600 m^3
tender budget:
3.5 billion lira
purpose:
administrative offices and service spaces annexed to the power station
structure:
earthquake-resistant r.c. frame; the ground floor structural grid has an interaxis of 4.8 m, while on the first floor the front pillars have an interaxis of 1.6 m; the 19.5 metre-span entrance portal is supported by 8 iron columns within the 2 glass-cement lanterns
principal materials:
external walls – coloured 20 x 20 x 40 cm concrete blocks horizontally interspersed with matching prefabricated 20 x 40 x 160 cm sandblasted concrete elements; glass cement straight and curved walls – 3190-type glass cement 19 x 19 x 8 cm bricks double soldered wall with rarefied air chamber: casings – painted aluminium sections and painted wooden doors; flooring and facing – artificial stone with spherogranite grey stoneware tiles and PVC
selected bibliography:
Domus, article by Francesco Moschini, no. 722, December 1990, pp. 38-47
Mario Bellini Architetture, Electa, 1988, pp. 54-61

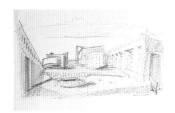

**Competition for the new
National Theatre
1986**

location:
Honmachi, Shibuya ward, Tokyo,
Japan
competition organizers:
Ministry of Construction
project:
1986
architect:
Mario Bellini, Mario Bellini
Associati Srl in collaboration with
Obayashi Co., Tokyo
design team:
T. Iwata, G. Origlia
theatre consultant
G. Cristini, Milan, head
stage-manager at the Teatro alla
Scala, Milan
model:
L. Morellato, Milan
floor area:
57,987 m^2
competition theme:
the new National Theatre
Complex including three different
sized theatres (Opera Theatre,
Middle Theatre, Small Theatre)
with various features and service
structures
selected bibliography:
*Entries in the Architectural
Competition for the New National
Theater, Tokyo, Japan*, Japan
Association for Construction
Government Buildings, 1986, p.
171
Mario Bellini Architetture, Electa,
1988, pp. 26-27
AT (Architecture Magazine), no.
10, October 1992

**The "Home Design"
exhibition
1986**

exhibition center:
Palazzo dell'Arte, Milan, Italy
client:
Ente Autonomo Triennale di
Milano
date:
18 January – 23 March 1986
**exhibition organization and
overall design:**
Mario Bellini, Mario Bellini
Associati Srl
scientific director:
G. Teyssot
curators:
M. De Michelis, M. Mosser, G.
Teyssot
design team:
G. Bonfanti, A. Torricella
graphic design:
I. Lupi, Milan
director of works:
G.P. Siemek, Milan
coordinator:
S. Sermisoni, Milan
surface area:
5,000 m^2
selected bibliography:
G. Teyssot (ed.), *Il progetto
domestico – la casa dell'uomo.
Archetipi e prototipi*, 2 vols.,
Electa-XVII Triennale di Milano,
1986, with writings by Mario
Bellini: "Introduzione", pp. 13-17,
(vol. *Saggi*) and "Pensate architetti
alla casa degli uomini" (with
G. Teyssot), pp. 9-13,
(vol. *Progetti*)
La Repubblica, 16 January 1986,
article by N. Aspesi
Panorama, 16 February 1986,
article by V. Gregotti, p. 19
International Herald Tribune, 8-9

February 1986, article by
K. Singleton
"La casa come l'abito è un mezzo
per comunicare", interview with
M. Bellini, *La mia casa*, no. 184,
January-February 1986
"La questione dell'abitazione"
(edited by S. Milesi), round table
during the exhibition "Il progetto
domestico alla XVII Triennale di
Milano", *Casabella*, no. 522,
March 1986, pp. 20-31
"Il progetto domestico", editorial
by M. Bellini, *Domus*, no. 671,
April 1986
Domus, no. 671, April 1986,
pp. 44-73
Mario Bellini Architetture, Electa,
1988, pp. 28-29

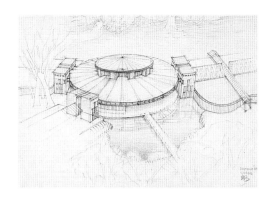

**Villa Erba International Congress and Exhibition Center
1986-90**

location:
Villa Erba Park, Cernobbio (Como), Italy
client:
Villa Erba SpA, Cernobbio (Como)
project:
from 1986
executed:
1987-90
architect:
Mario Bellini, Mario Bellini Associati Srl
design team:
G. Bonfanti, R. Cipolletta
collaborators:
M. Angiolini, P. Lissi, M. Parravicini, G. Pigni
project management:
Villa Erba SpA
structural engineers:
L. Antonietti, Milan – dome: M. Locatelli, Milan
installations:
Manens Intertecnica Srl, Verona
electrical engineering:
Elettromeccanica Galli Italo SpA, Erba (Como)
mechanical engineering:
Consorzio Temporaneo d'Imprese IGEIT Srl, Cesano Maderno (Milan)-F.d.S. Impianti SpA, Milano-Fratelli Panzeri Impianti SpA, Gironico (Como)
quantity surveyors:
Società Progettazioni Integrali SpA, Milan
director of works:
Mario Bellini Associati Srl
artistic director:
Mario Bellini Associati Srl

contractors:
Associazione Temporanea d'Imprese Nessi & Maiocchi SpA, Como; Carboncini & C. Sas, Lomazzo (Como)
site area:
65,000 m^2
floor area:
14,000 m^2
volume:
56,000 m^3
tender budget:
45 billion lira
purpose:
the central-plan pavilion can be used for exhibitions, concerts, congresses, and has a seating capacity of about 1200; the three wings connected to it form the actual exhibition structure
structure:
the central-plan pavilion is built with a steel frame hung from three reinforced concrete towers; the exhibition wings are made up of a regular steel structural grid
service installations:
the installations and service areas are located on the basement floor of the central pavilion; situated in the central pavilion are the technical installations; all the systems distribution networks are underneath the floors of the central and secondary corridor
principal materials:
walls – sintered cement blocks with pink ochre paste colouring to obtain the same colour as the facade of the existing Villa; the service towers are faced in a vertical travertine pattern; painted iron open girders along the front perimeter of the three wings and copper gutters; all the frames (greenhouses, undulating wall,

skylights, entrances) are made from painted aluminium sections; the main passageways are covered by glazed roofing, whereas the transverse passages have lean-to roofing consisting of opaline white sheets; flooring in the exhibition pavilions – grey lava stone and travertine

selected bibliography:
Mario Bellini Architetture, Electa, 1988, pp. 62-71
Frames, no. 4, July-September 1989, pp. 36-41
Exporre, no. 3, March 1990, p. 12
Vetro-Spazio, no. 18, September 1990, pp. 10-16
L'Arca, no. 44, December 1990, p. 106
Euro Pronto, vol.1, no. 1, 1991, pp. 21-27
A x A, no. 2, September 1991, pp. 4-11
Costruzioni Metalliche, no. 2, 1991, pp. 65-73
L'Architettura della tecnologia, E.A. Fiera di Bologna, 1992, pp. 35-53
A + U, no. 260, May 1992, pp. 86-95
AT (Architecture Magazine), no. 10, October 1992, pp. 19-23
Blueprint Extra, monographic issue, 1993
"La serra dei congressi", article by E. Morteo, *Abitare*, no. 321, September 1993, pp. 186-193

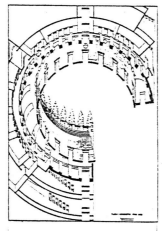

**Design for the "Mario Bellini
Designer" exhibition
1987**

exhibition center:
The Museum of Modern Art, New
York, USA
client:
The Museum of Modern Art,
Department of Architecture and
Design, New York, USA
date:
24 June – 15 September 1987
architect:
Mario Bellini, Mario Bellini Ass. Srl
design team:
A. Torricella
curator:
Cara McCarty, Assistant Curator,
Department of Architecture and
Design, The Museum of Modern Art
surface area:
400 m^2
principal materials:
painted plasterboard for the
arcade structure; stands and
pedestals – painted wood
selected bibliography:
Mario Bellini designer, (edited by
Cara McCarty), exhibition
catalogue, The Museum of
Modern Art, New York, 1987
Industrial Design, May-June 1987
The New York Times, article by
Susan Slezin and Patricia Leigh
Brown, 25 June 1987
Corriere della Sera article by
Cesare de Seta, 27 June 1987
Philadelphia Inquirer, article by
Thomas Hine, 23 August 1987
Il Sole 24 Ore, article by Renzo
Zorzi, 23 August 1987, p. 14
The New York Times, article by
John Russel, 28 August 1987
Mario Bellini Architetture, Electa,
1988, pp. 30-31

**Yokohama Business Park:
Master Plan, Plaza and
Concourse
1987-91**

location:
Godo-cho Hodogaya-ku
Yokohama, Japan
client:
Nomura Real Estate Dev.,
Tokyo
project:
from 1987
executed:
1987-91
architect:
Mario Bellini, Mario Bellini
Associati Srl
design team:
A. Esposito
collaborators:
O. De Luca, E. Gueli, C. Malnati,
A. Mazzullo, R. Sturgeon, N.
Terakawa
project management:
YBP Design Room
(Nomura Real Estate
Dev.-Obayashi Co.)
structural engineers:
YBP Design Room
project impianti:
YBP Design Room
quantity surveyors:
Obayashi Co., Tokyo
director of works:
YBP Design Room
artistic director:
Mario Bellini Associati Srl
contractors:
Obayashi Co., Tokyo
site area:
71,056 m^2
floor area:
230,000 m^2
tender budget:
600 billion yen

awards:
1990
GID Prize at the 1st Good Interior
Design Competition (Japan)
Second SDA Prize at the 24th
SDA Prize (Japan)
1991
6th Yokohama Machizukuri
Kourousha Prize (Japan)
9th Nashop Lighting Contest
Theme Prize (Japan)
Prize at the 12th NSG Shop
& Interior Design Contest
(Japan)
Kensetsusho (Ministry of
Construction) Machizukuri
Korousha Prize (Japan)
Shorei Prize at the 25th SDA Prize
(Japan)
First Prize at the 36th Kanagawa
Kenchiku Concours (Japan)
1992
4th Yokohama Machinami Keikan
(Cityscope) Prize (Japan)
purpose:
public spaces and facilities for the
Business Park
structure and principal materials:
circular wall crowning the
pool-square – exposed r.c. with
horizontal travertine strip inserts;
the concentric rings of walls
forming the hillside are made
from brick-red coloured cement;
the square-theatre is paved in a
circular pattern with cement
slabs and small blocks; the
trellis-work is made of painted
galvanized steel
selected bibliography:
Mario Bellini Architetture, Electa,
1988, pp. 74-83
Nikkei Architecture, no. 5, 1990,
pp. 90-96
Shinkenchiku, no. 6, 1990,
pp. 289-295

Shinkenchiku, no. 1, 1991,
pp. 360-363
Shoten Kenchiku, no. 1, vol. 36,
January 1991, pp. 174-179
Nikkei Architecture, no. 2, 1991,
pp. 186-191
Kenchiku Gaho, no. 226, vol. 27,
November 1991, pp. 77-85
Japan Landscape, no. 19, 1991,
pp. 78-83
YBP-Works, Nomura Real Estate,
1992

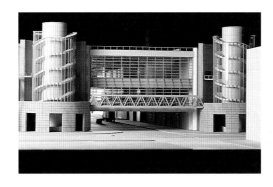

**Extension to the Portello
Sud area at the Milan Trade
Fair
1987-ongoing**

location:
Viale Scarampo, Milan, Italy
client:
Ente Autonomo Fiera di Milano
project:
from 1987
executed:
1993-ongoing
architect:
Mario Bellini, Mario Bellini
Associati Srl
design team:
P. Allen, G. Bonfanti, G. Filiputti, C.
Malnati, V. Prina
collaborators:
M. Adriante, M. Barda, E.
Beorchia, E. Bruschi, G.
Cappelletti, P. Curti, O. De Luca, S.
Felton, A. Fiorentini, S. Grioni, D.
Haddock, L. Lee, G. Mbaied, G.
Pigni, V. Samarati, M.
Santagostino, C. Sattler, P. Seria,
D. Severo, R. Simeoni, A.
Tiraboschi, D. Vianello, M.
Zanichelli
model:
L. Morellato, Milan
project management:
Fiera Milano technical director,
A. Vettese
structural engineers:
Redesco Srl, Milan, G. Giuliani
installations:
Intertecno SpA, Milan,
P. Cattaneo
quantity surveyors:
Società Progettazioni Integrali
SpA, Milan – Fiera Milano
technical management with
external consultation from Protek
Srl, Milan

overall supervision of works:
Fiera Milano technical director,
A. Vettese
director of works:
TEKNE Srl, Milan – ELC
Electroconsult, Milan
artistic director:
M. Bellini, R. Cipolletta, C.
Malnati, G. Pigni
contractors:
C.M.C., Ravenna – Frabboni,
Bologna – Maltauro, Vicenza –
Recchi, Turin – Pizzarotti, Parma –
CGC Enterprise, Saint André C.
(France) – Italtel Telesis, Milan –
Kone Corporation, Helsinki
(Finland)
floor area:
106,000 m^2
volume:
1,127,000 m^3
tender budget:
300 billion lira
purpose:
exhibition pavilions and support
functions integrated to the
present Milan Fair precincts; the
monumental Tympanum placed
above the terminal head of the
last pavilion houses the Fair's
reception functions
structure:
the structural plan proposes the
use of precast *in situ* octagonal
pillars, 120 × 120 cm and 23 m
high, set at the intersections of a
20 × 20 m square grid; the
horizontal structures at 15 m high
are formed by precast *in situ*
orthotropic slabs, 20 × 20 m,
raised by hydraulic jacks; the
horizontal structures at 7 m and
23 m are built with T-beams and
prefabricated joists cast *in situ* in
20 × 20 m movable moulds – they
are raised by hydraulic jacks; the

tympanum consists of a steel
frame with spatial plan; the
circular stairs have an *in situ*
exposed r.c core containing the
lift shafts; vehicular ramps –
precast r.c.; heavy transport ramp
– *in situ* r.c.
The elevation on Via Tranchedini
presents a two-storey high arcade
formed by r.c. trusses and pillars,
as is the pergola frame
principal materials:
base – precast concrete vertical
panels (Ceppo Gentile type) 2.5 m
wide; their washed and
bush-hammered surface
highlights the stone aggregate of
the concrete mix; the pavilion –
precast panels with sandblasted
finishing of very fine yellow
marble grit; metal structures –
silver-coloured ferromica paint
frames – medium grey RAL 7001
painted metal
selected bibliography:
Mario Bellini Architetture, Electa,
1988, pp. 102-113
*Milano. Architetture per la città.
1980-1990*, Editoriale Domus,
1989, pp. 116-119
Exporre, no. 3, March 1990, p. 8
Domus, report by Ermanno
Ranzani, pp. 25-41, article by
Franco Purini, "Fiera di Milano. Sul
progetto Bellini", pp. 42-43, no.
728, June 1991
AT (Architecture Magazine), no.
10, October 1992
"Una nuova Fiera a Milano",
Ufficio Stile, no. 3, May-June 1995

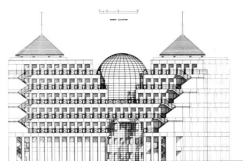

Competition for the Ryoma Sakamoto Memorial Hall 1988

location:
Katsurahama Park, Kochi City, Japan
competition organizers:
Ryoma 150th Anniversary Projects Executive Committee, Japan Academic Society of Construction
project:
1988
architect:
Mario Bellini, Mario Bellini Associati Srl in collaboration with Obayashi Co., Tokyo
design team:
P. Lissi, E. Ranzani, V. Samarati
collaborators:
G. Mbaied
site area:
7,826 m^2
floor area:
1,413 m^2 (861 m^2 above ground + 552 m^2 basement)
tender budget:
550 million yen
competition theme:
Mausoleum in memory of R. Sakamoto, a Japanese national hero
structure:
precast *in situ* r.c.
principal materials:
Outer shell, stairway and entrance courtyard in exposed r.c.; inner space – red plaster
selected bibliography:
Mario Bellini Architetture, Electa, 1988, pp. 86-91

Tokyo Design Center 1988-92

location:
25-19 Higashi Gotanda 5-chome, Shinagawa-ku, Tokyo, Japan
client:
Sowa Shoji Co. Ltd., Tokyo
project:
from 1988
executed:
1989-92
architect:
Mario Bellini, Mario Bellini Associati Srl
design team:
P. Lissi, C. Malnati, V. Samarati
model:
D. Gelati, Milan
equestrian sculpture:
Mimmo Paladino, Padula (Benevento)
executive architects:
Mario Bellini Associati Srl – Obayashi Co., Tokyo
project management:
Takatoshi Ide, Artechnic Inc., Tokyo
project producer:
Artechnic Inc., Takatoshi Ide, Tokyo
structural engineers:
Obayashi Co., Tokyo
installations:
Obayashi Co., Tokyo
quantity surveyors:
Obayashi Co., Tokyo
director of works:
Obayashi Co., Tokyo
artistic director:
Mario Bellini Associati Srl
contractors:
Obayashi Co., Tokyo
site area:
1,958 m^2
floor area:
11,874 m^2
volume:
41,000 m^3
tender budget:
6 billion yen
awards:
1992
Designers (3rd division: showroom and other commercial premises except for the shops) (Japan)
1993
Building Contractors Society Prize, Tokyo (Japan)
purpose:
multistorey building for furniture showrooms (9 floors above ground – h 34.5 m – and two basement levels); the reception and cafeteria are located on levels 2 and 3; the two-level exhibition hall is in the basement; the client's offices are on the eighth and ninth floors
structure:
steel and *in situ* exposed r.c.
principal materials:
the exterior is clad in precast exposed concrete panels with inlaid travertine fascias; gallery walls – travertine; wide access stairway – grey lava; flooring – Carrara marble and parquet; door and window frames – light grey painted aluminium; the roof pyramids containing the air-conditioning plants are faced with light grey painted aluminium slats
selected bibliography:
Nikkei Architecture, no. 4, 1992, pp. 164-169
Shinkenchiku, no. 5, 1992, pp. 223-234
Shoten Kenchiku, no. 5, vol. 37, May 1992, pp. 170-179
FP, no. 49, 1992, pp. 61-65
JA, no. 3, July 1992, pp. 180-191
AT (Architecture Magazine), no. 10, October 1992
Domus, article by Fumihiko Maki, no. 743, November 1992, pp. 36-43
Nikkei Architecture, no. 2, 1993, pp. 174-175
GA Japan, no. 3, Spring 1993, pp. 104-107

**Two Residential Buildings
1988-96**

location:
Via Madonnina – Via Fiori Chiari,
Milan, Italy
client:
CEID ITALY – Fondiaria SpA,
Firenze
project:
from 1988
executed:
1991-96
architect:
Mario Bellini, Mario Bellini
Associati Srl
design team:
V. Samarati, C. Malnati
collaborators:
M. Adriante, P. H. Allen
model:
L. Morellato, Milan
project management:
Gestioni Arcotecnica, Milan
geotechnics:
Studio Geotecnico Italiano
structural engineers:
(basement levels) Italprogetti,
Milan
(above ground levels) Sorgato,
Milan
installations:
Studio Bozino Resmini, Milan
quantity surveyors:
Gestioni Arcotecnica, Milan
director of works:
A. Zanichelli, Bologna
artistic director:
Mario Bellini Associati Srl
contractors:
Associazione Temporanea
d'Imprese ELSE SpA-Ranza
SpA, Milan – Procogen,
Firenze
lot areas:
720 m^2

floor area:
housing 1,130 m^2
car park 4,146 m^2
volume:
housing 3,729 m^3
car park 10,365 m^3
tender budget:
15 billion lira
awards:
commended in *Milano Progetti
1989*, Commissione edilizia del
Comune di Milano.
purpose:
multistorey residential buildings
(4 floors above ground) with
4-level basement garage (108
parking lots)
structure:
steel and r.c.
principal materials:
fronts – plaster with light yellow
mock marble; bases composed
of gilded bush-hammered
Valmalenco stone; frames –
painted wood; roofs – copper
selected bibliography:
Mario Bellini Architetture, Electa,
1988, pp. 94-101
*Milano. Architetture per la città.
1980-1990*, Editoriale Domus,
1989, p. 62
Milano Progetti Ottantanove,
Comune di Milano, 1988
Casa Oggi, no. 248, April 1995,
pp. 30-31
"La mia città preferita", *Town and
Design,* April 1991

**Design for Housing
1989-92**

location:
Via Varese, Milan, Italy
client:
Gyante Srl, Milan
project:
1989-92
architect:
Mario Bellini, Mario Bellini
Associati Srl
design team:
E. Bruschi, E. Gueli, C. Malnati
collaborators:
M. Adriante
model:
L. Morellato, Milan
site area:
950 m^2
floor area:
1,048 m^2
volume:
3,450 m^3
tender budget:
3 billion lira
purpose:
three-storey housing with
three-level underground parking
structure:
in situ r.c.
principal materials:
the fronts in Via Varese and
towards the garden are clad in
Ceppo di Poltragno slabs,
whereas the set-back volumes of
the top floors are faced with
copper panels; the elliptic wall
delimiting the central courtyard is
plastered with red silicate marble
grit; bronze frames

**Design for Motorway Service Areas
1989**

location:
various service areas on the
Italian motorway network
client:
Autogrill SpA, Milan
project:
1989
executed:
being planned
architect:
Mario Bellini, Mario Bellini
Associati Srl
design team:
E. Bruschi, V. Samarati
collaborators:
M. Adriante, A. Tiraboschi
(computer graphics)
model:
Mario Bellini Associati Srl
floor area:
2,400 m^2
tender budget:
4 billion lira
purpose:
catering services and facilities for
the sale of miscellaneous goods
for Italian motorway users
structure:
r.c.; the glasshouse volume has a
boxed steel rib frame
principal materials:
the cone containing the bar is
faced with polished steel panels;
the other volumes are exposed
r.c. and are differentiated by their
colours according to cubist
schemes; the glasshouse volume
has glazed insulating panels
selected bibliography:
Domus, article by Ermanno
Ranzani, no. 755, December
1993, pp. 36-41

**Competition by invitation
for the new Bayer Italia
Center
1989**

location:
Milan, Italy
client:
Bayer Italy SpA, Milan
project:
1989
architect:
Mario Bellini, Mario Bellini
Associati Srl
design team:
P. Azzolini, A. Esposito. C. Malnati
collaborators:
E. Beorchia, E. Bruschi, D. Farris,
E. Gueli, A. Incerti, P. Lissi, V.
Samarati, P. Vieira Mallen, M.
Zanibelli
office planning consultants:
DEGW, London
model:
L. Morellato, Milan
structural engineers:
Ove Arup & Partners, London
consultant engineers:
Ove Arup & Partners
site area:
15,000 m^2
floor area:
49,913 m^2
21,771 m^2 underground car parks
volume:
199,652 m^3
tender budget:
120 billion lira
purpose:
head office for Bayer Italy and
sister companies Agfa and Miles
structure:
r.c. towers; crowning trusses –
precompressed r.c.; office floor
systems hung by metal tie-beams
from steel roof trusses

principal materials:
towers faced in
terracotta-coloured sandstone;
roof trusses – precompressed
exposed r.c. with steel stays and
copper covering; office blocks –
external steel tie-beams, steel
storey fascia and sun-shades;
windows – anodized aluminium
frames and glass with low
emissivity

**Cassina Japan Showroom
1989**

location:
Minami Aoyama Collezione
Building, Tokyo, Japan
client:
Cassina Japan Inc., Tokyo
project:
1989
executed:
1990
architect:
Mario Bellini, Mario Bellini
Associati Srl
design team:
G. Bonfanti
collaborators:
M. Parravicini
painting:
Sandro Chia, Montalcino (Siena)
surface area:
300 m^2
tender budget:
70 million yen
purpose:
Cassina showroom
structure:
the double wall and staircase
have a metal structure
principal materials:
the double wall is clad in
cement-based panels with
engraved lines reproducing large
hewn stones; the stairs are faced
in galvanized metal panels;
reception desk – sandblasted
glass; finishing – Pompeii-red
encaustic; floors – grey granite
and cherry wood
selected bibliography:
Nikkei Architecture, no. 11, 1989,
pp. 248-252
Shoten Kenchiku, no. 12, vol. 34,
December 1989, pp. 194-195
Icon, no. 1, vol. 21, 1990, pp.

88-92
Interior Design, December 1991,
pp. 86-89
International Interiors III, edited by
Lucy Bullivant, Thames and
Hudson, 1992, pp. 182-185

**Risonare – Vivre Club
Complex
1989-92**

location:
Kobuchizawa, Yamanashi, Japan
client:
Vivre, Nichii Co. Ltd., Osaka
project:
from 1989
executed:
1991-92
architect:
Mario Bellini, Mario Bellini
Associati Srl
design team:
L. Buti, M. Matsuno, A. Mazzullo
collaborators:
E. Bruschi, C. Costa, E. Gueli, C.
Malnati
executive project:
Mario Bellini Associati Srl –
Takeda Associates Architects,
Osaka
interior design:
Mario Bellini Associati Srl –
Giorgio Origlia, Milan (guest
rooms)
model:
L. Morellato, Milan
project management:
Takeda Associates Architects,
Osaka
structural engineers:
Gendai Sekkei, Osaka
installations:
Takeda Associates Architects,
Osaka
quantity surveyors:
Takeda Associates Architects,
Osaka
director of works:
Takeda Associates Architects,
Osaka
artistic director:
Mario Bellini Associati Srl

contractors:
Nissan Construction Co., Ltd.,
Tokyo
site area:
71,379 m^2
floor area:
38,159 m^2
tender budget:
26 billion yen
purpose:
tourist center with 200 rooms
consisting of residences, hotel,
restaurants, conference halls,
discotheque, theatre/auditorium,
health center and a large covered
swimming-pool with artificial
wave motion
structure:
in situ r.c.; terraced cover to the
swimming-pool – steel trusses;
the large side glazed structure
has its own steel frame as does
the hotel glazing
principal materials:
the residence – sand-white
coloured fronts; arcaded base –
grooved exposed concrete; hotel
– sprayed dark-red fronts with
horizontal grooving; hotel and
residence terrace pergolas –
wood; service volumes –
aluminium sheet cladding
selected bibliography:
Nikkei Architetture, no. 8, 1992,
pp. 112-125
Shinkenchiku, no. 9, 1992, pp.
235-248
Shoten Kenchiku, no. 9,
September 1992, pp. 170-181
GA Japan, no. 3, Spring 1993, pp.
150-157

Invited Consultation for "Berlin Morgen: Ideen für das Herz einer Großstadt" 1990

location:
Berlin, Germany
organizers:
Deutsches Architektur Museum in collaboration with the *Frankfurter Allgemeine Zeitung*
project:
1990
architect:
Mario Bellini, Mario Bellini Associati Srl
design team:
C. Bellini, A. Esposito, D. Severo, L. Viti
competition theme:
proposals for a new overall plan for the central area of Berlin
selected bibliography:
Berlin Morgen: Ideen für das Herz einer Großstadt, ed.
V. M. Lampugnani and
M. Mönninger (exhibition catalogue), Deutsches Architektur Museum, Frankfurt and Hatje Verlag, Stuttgart, 1991, pp. 88-93
Domus, no. 725, March 1991, pp. 54-63
Frankfurter Allgemeine Zeitung, no. 4, January 1991
"Mario Bellini. Revitalising a multiple heart", *Architectural Design*, monographic issue, 1991
"Berlin tomorrow. International Architectural Visions", no. 92, published as a part of *Architectural Design*, 1991, pp. 20-29

Studio for Mario Bellini Associati Srl 1990-93

location:
Piazza Arcole 4, Milan
client:
Mario Bellini Associati Srl
project:
1990-93
executed:
1991-93
architect:
Mario Bellini, Mario Bellini Associati Srl
design team:
G. Bonfanti, E. Bruschi, C. Malnati
collaborators:
M. Angiolini, E. Beorchia, E. Gueli, L. Morandi, M. Parravicini
structural engineers:
R. Ercoli, Milan
installations:
Pioggia Srl, Milan
quantity surveyors:
Mario Bellini Associati Srl
artistic director:
Mario Bellini Associati Srl
contractors:
COGED, Cologno al Serio (Bergamo)
floor area:
1,600 m^2
volume:
6,400 m^3
tender budget:
4 billion lira
purpose:
architectural and design studio
structure:
load-bearing walls – brick; floors – concrete brickwork; roofs – galvanized steel trusses
principal materials:
exteriors: plaster coloured at mortar stage, painted aluminium

frames; base and sills – gneiss; trellis-work – galvanized steel
selected bibliography:
Eciffo, vol. 27, 1995, pp. 10-26

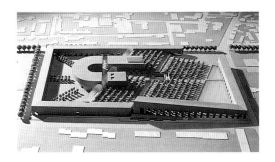

Invited Consultation for the San Donato Milanese Town Center 1991

location:
San Donato Milanese (Milan), Italy
client:
SNAM SpA in collaboration with the Comune di San Donato Milanese
project:
1991
architect:
Mario Bellini, Mario Bellini Associati Srl
design team:
M. Angiolini, G. Bonfanti, R. Cipolletta, C. Malnati
collaborators:
M. Parravicini
model:
L. Morellato, Milan
site area:
131,700 m^2
floor area:
110,500 m^2
volume:
365,000 m^3
competition theme:
the creation of a multi-purpose town center to include housing, services, shops, public and cultural facilities, and underground parking
structure:
r.c.; galleries – steel pillars and girders
principal materials:
arcade – stone cladding; the upper, residential, floors have plastered fronts; the large sloping front has terraced gardens; the gallery is glazed
selected bibliography:
"Centro città" San Donato

Milanese (catalogue), Comune di San Donato Milanese, 1992
Quinto Miglio, no. 4, April 1992
Il Cittadino, no. 5, May 1992
AT (Architecture Magazine), no. 10, October 1992

Ideas Competition for a Business Center in the Garibaldi-Repubblica Area 1991

location:
the Garibaldi-Repubblica area, Milan, Italy
competition organizers:
Comune di Milano-Associazione degli Interessi Metropolitani (AIM)
project:
1991
architects:
Mario Bellini, Mario Bellini Associati Srl with Marco Romano, Milan
collaborators:
C. Bellini, E. Bruschi, G. Cappelletti, A. Esposito, C. Malnati, L. Viti, M. Zanibelli
model:
L. Morellato, Milan
floor area:
196,000 m^2
volume:
657,261 m^3
competition theme:
the construction of an important Milan business center with significant public, City Council and Regional buildings in an area mostly owned by the City Council situated between the Garibaldi railway station and the Piazza della Repubblica
selected bibliography:
Progetti per Milano – Concorso di idee per il polo direzionale-finanziario nell'area Garibaldi-Repubblica, catalogue, Abitare Segesta-Cataloghi, 1992
AT (Architecture Magazine), no. 10, October 1992

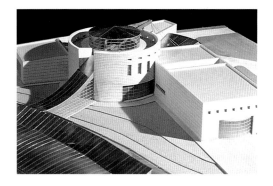

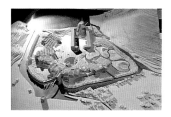

**Primary School
1991-95**

location:
Via Massimo d'Azeglio, Giussano
(Milan), Italy
client:
Comune di Giussano
project:
from 1991
executed:
1992-95
architect:
Mario Bellini, Mario Bellini
Associati Srl
design team:
G. Bonfanti, R. Cipolletta
collaborators:
M. Angiolini, G. Mbaied, M.
Parravicini, G. Pigni
model:
L. Morellato, Milan
structural engineers:
A. Donadio, SPS Studio
Associato, Milan; lamellar wood
structures – R. Bramani, Habitat
Legno, Edolo (Brescia)
installations:
Sinergo, Milan, P. Junginger
(electrical) – Primatec, Seregno
(Milan), C.Gatti (mechanical)
quantity surveyors:
Mario Bellini Associati Srl
director of works:
A. Cendali, Giussano (Milan)
artistic director:
Mario Bellini Associati Srl
contractors:
Progetti & Costruzioni SpA, Milan;
Moncada Costruzioni Srl,
Agrigento; Habitat Legno,
Edolo (Brescia); Carvoz,
Cologno Monzese (Milan);
ETS Srl, Limbiate (Milan);
Tecnoelettrica, Ciserano
(Bergamo)

site area:
9,500 m^2
floor area:
2,820 m^2
volume:
10,585 m^3
tender budget:
4.5 billion lira
purpose:
Primary school with 15
classrooms, 7 special teaching
rooms, gymnasium, assembly
room, dining hall and
administrative offices
structure:
classrooms – r.c. with lamellar
wood roof beams; central
cylinder – r.c.; gymnasium, dining
room and assembly room – r.c.
principal materials:
in the classroom block the fronts
are completely glazed, while the
frames are painted aluminium;
the gymnasium, dining room and
hall – exposed concrete
alternated with unfaced brick
course; roof – aluminium-finished
lamellar wood

**Design for the Goshikidai
Marine Resort Complex
1992-93**

location:
Goshikidai, Island of Shikoku,
Kagawa-ken, Japan
client:
Nichii Co., Ltd., Osaka
project:
1992-93
architect:
Mario Bellini, Mario Bellini
Associati Srl
design team:
C. Bellini, L. Buti, O. De Luca, P.
Lissi, M. Matsuno
collaborators:
A. Tiraboschi (computer graphics)
model:
Mario Bellini Associati Srl
site area:
250,000 m^2
floor area:
65,000 m^2
car parks-services 15,000 m^2
tender budget:
40 million yen
purpose:
a marina and tourist resort
comprising residences, shopping
center, sports facilities, cultural
and entertainment amenities,
tourist port and car parks

 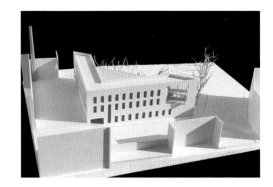

**Design for the Dubai Creek Complex
1994**

location:
Beniyas Road, Dubai Creek New Marina, Deira, Dubai, United Arab Emirates
client:
Al-Rostamani Group of Companies, Dubai
project:
1994
architect:
Mario Bellini, Mario Bellini Associati Srl
design team:
L. Buti
collaborators:
N. Artuso, E. Brandinelli, M. De Ferrari, F. De Vita
model:
L. Morellato, Milan
site area:
3,952 m^2
floor area:
28,200 m^2
underground car park – 7,700 m^2
volume:
103,100 m^3
underground car park 24,640 m^3
tender budget:
35 million US dollars
purpose:
commercial center (23 floors above ground) with a two-floor arcaded base including residences (the half-wave building) and offices (the prism building)
structure:
r.c.
principal materials:
arcade and office building – red terracotta-coloured sandstone finishing, painted aluminium

frames, brushed stainless steel sun screens; apartment-block curved front is faced with anodized silver aluminium; hanging swimming pool finished with anodized silver aluminium

**New branch for the Schmidtbank and redevelopment of the surrounding area with the creation of a new square
1994-ongoing**

location:
Albert Einstein Strasse-Johannisplatz, Limbach-Oberfrohna, Germany
client:
Schmidtbank-Zentrale Hof, Germany
project:
1994
executed:
ongoing
architect:
Mario Bellini, Mario Bellini Associati Srl
design team:
L. Buti
collaborators:
M. Adriante
executive project:
Mario Bellini Associati Srl – Bertsch-Friedrich Kalcher Dipl. Ing. Freie Architekten BDA, Stuttgart
model:
Mario Bellini Associati Srl
project management:
Bertsch Friedrich Kalcher Dipl. Ing. Freie Architekten BDA
structural engineers:
Ingenieurbüro Stapff, Forsthuber + Partner, Stuttgart
installations:
Ingenieurbüro Walter Scheer, Stuttgart
quantity surveyors:
Bertsch Friedrich Kalcher Architekten BDA
site area:
4,179 m^2 (with square)

floor area:
2,771 m^2 (with car park)
volume:
11,515 m^3
tender budget:
9.5 million German marks
purpose:
bank, offices, coffee shop and underground car park
structure:
r.c. and steel
principal materials:
L-shaped building – external and internal walls are made of red brick; triangular building – steel fronts glazed with Infrastop Neutral; floors – gneiss and carpets

**International Competition
for the Yokohama
International Port Terminal
1994**

location:
Yokohama, Japan
competition organizers:
City of Yokohama
project:
1994
architect:
Mario Bellini, Mario Bellini
Associati Srl
design team:
M. Matsuno, Mario Bellini
Associati Srl – Mitsubishi Estate
Co., Ltd – Ove Arup & Partners
Japan Limited – Artechnic Inc.,
Tokyo – Mec Design International,
Tokyo – J-Tec Corp., Tokyo
computer graphics:
Juraj Hidveghy, Articrom Srl, Milan
site area:
33,000 m^2
floor area:
48,000 m^2
tender budget:
23 billion yen
purpose:
international port terminal
structure:
steel and r.c.
principal materials:
steel; aluminium roof; glazed
fronts; base – exposed r.c.

**Exhibition Designs for
"The Renaissance from
Brunelleschi to
Michelangelo. The
representation of
architecture"
1994-95**

exhibition centers:
Palazzo Grassi, Venice, Italy;
Musée National des Monuments
Français, Paris, France; Altes
Museum, Berlin, Germany
clients:
Palazzo Grassi SpA, Venice;
Musée National des Monuments
Français, Paris; Kunstbibliothek,
Berlin
date:
1994-95
design and coordination:
Mario Bellini, Mario Bellini
Associati Srl
design team:
G. Bonfanti, G. Cappelletti
collaborators:
R. Cipolletta
**scientific committee
coordinators:**
Henry Millon, Vittorio Magnago
Lampugnani
graphic design:
I. Lupi, Milan
lighting:
Mario Bellini – A. Pollice, Milan
surface areas:
Palazzo Grassi, Venice, 1,800 m^2
Musée National des Monuments
Français, Paris, 1,000 m^2
Altes Museum, Berlin, 1,440 m^2
tender budget:
Palazzo Grassi, 900 million lira
Musée National des Monuments
Français, 350 million lira
Altes Museum, 500 million lira

selected bibliography:
Financial Times, article by Colin
Amery, April 1994, pp. 16-17
Abitare, no. 330, June 1994, pp.
182-189
Corriere della Sera, article by C.
De Seta, 5 November 1994
"Un allestimento di luce per le
architetture del Rinascimanto",
Exporre, no. 20, June 1994
Bauwelt, no. 20, 20 May 1994

Appendices

List of architectural works

Executed works

1960
*Exhibition Design for the
"Compasso d'Oro" Award*,
Palazzo Reale, Milan, Italy
with Italo Lupi
1961
*Exhibition Design for the
"Compasso d'Oro" Award
Retrospective "Italia '61"*,
Turin, Italy
with Bruno Munari
1965
Kindergarten, Paderno Dugnano
(Milan), Italy
with Marco Romano
1967-68
GESCAL Quarter, Paderno
Dugnano (Milan), Italy
with Giovanni e Marco Romano
1968
Restaurant "Il Tondorante",
Bard (Aosta), Italy
1969
Cassina Showroom, Via Durini,
Milan, Italy
1978-87
*Technical and Commercial
Institute – "Rolando da Piazzola"*,
Piazzola sul Brenta (Padova), Italy
1982
Interdecor Showroom, Tokyo,
Japan
*Restoration of the Pestalozza
Garden*, Milan, Italy
with Pietro Porcinai
1984-87
*Exhibition Designs for "The
Treasures of San Marco"* (*)
1984-88
Offices and Industrial Complex,
Milan, Italy (*)
1985
*Italian Pavillion of Science
and Technology*, Expo '85,

Tsukuba, Japan
1985-90
*Offices and Landscaping for the
Cassano D'Adda Thermoelectric
Power Station*, Milan, Italy (*)
1986
"The Home Design" exhibition,
at the XVIIth Triennale di Milano,
Milan, Italy (*)
1986-90
*Villa Erba International Congress
and Exhibition Center*, Cernobbio
(Como), Italy (*)
1987
*Design for the "Mario Bellini
Designer" exhibition*, The
Museum of Modern Art,
New York (*)
1987-91
Yokohama Business Park,
Yokohama, Japan (*)
1988
*Overall project and design of the
Italian section in the exhibition
"The cities of the world and the
future of the metropolis"*, XVIIth
Triennale di Milano, Milan, Italia
1988-92
Tokyo Design Center, Tokyo,
Japan (*)
1988-96
Two Residential Buildings, Via
Madonnina-Via Fiori Chiari, Milan,
Italy (*)
1989
*Exhibition design for "Italian Art in
the 20th Century"*, Royal Academy
of Art, London, United Kingdom
Cassina Japan Showroom, Tokyo,
Japan (*)
1989-92
Risonare-Vivre Club Complex,
Kobuchizawa, Japan (*)
1991
*Living space for a Japanese
family*, "Good Living Show",

Tokyo, Japan
1991-95
Primary School, Giussano (Milan),
Italy (*)
1992
Rosenthal Showroom, permanent
exhibition space, Frankfurt Fair,
Germany
1993
Ideal living space, Frankfurt Fair,
Germany
*Studio for Mario Bellini Associati
Srl*, Milan, Italy (*)
1994-95
*Exhibition Designs for "The
Renaissance from Brunelleschi to
Michelangelo. The representation
of architecture"* (*)

Ongoing projects

Al Ahlia Commercial Center,
competition by invitation, Dubai,
United Arab Emirates
Dubai Creek Complex, Dubai,
United Arab Emirates (*)
*Dubai Creek Bridge –
Multipurpose Complex*, Dubai,
United Arab Emirates
Re-landscaping of Mushrif Park,
Dubai, United Arab Emirates
*Presidential Palace Complex – the
Citadel*, Moscow, Russia

Non executed works

1963-65
*New light prefabrication building
system for schools and housing*,
with Marco Romano
1964
*New town center at Paderno
Dugnano (Milan)*, Italy
with Marco Romano

1967

New building for the Faculty of Computer Science, Ivrea (Turin), Italy
with Marco Romano
Heavy prefabrication system
with Marco Romano

1968

New housing typology, for the Società Umanitaria
with Marco Romano

1970

Research on hospital typologies for large urban centers, commissioned by the Consiglio Nazionale delle Ricerche (CNR)

1971

High School, Bresso (Milan), Italy
with Marco Romano

1972

Hospital Complex, Piacenza, Italy
with architects Carozzi e Rozzi

1978

Building and type system for primary and high schools, accepted as a project type by the Lombardy Region
in collaboration with the contractors Del Favero

1979

New school typology with solar energy systems, award-winning entry in the competition "Il Sole e l'Habitat" organized by Istituto Nazionale di Architettura

1982

Villa on the island of Mustique, the Caribbean

1984

Conversion of the electric exchanges and restoration of the buildings, bed and sluices of the Naviglio Canal, Paderno d'Adda (Milan), Italy
Piazza Anita Garibaldi arrangement, Baggio (Milan), Italy

1985

Urban plan for Via Veneto and new verandah for the Caffè Carpano, Rome, Italy

1987

Television Exchange Center, Shanghai, China

1989

Aem heating station, offices and facilities, Milan, Italy

1989

Design for Motorway Service Areas, Italy (*)

1989-92

Housing, Via Varese, Milan, Italy

1991

Housing and office tower, Osaka, Japan
Restoration and redevelopment of historic buildings and areas in the city of Faenza and the restoration of the International Ceramics Museum, Faenza (Forlì), Italy
Restoration and transformation of the Este Castle at Ferrara into a museum of history and culture, Ferrara, Italy
Master Plan for the San Sebastian de Los Reyes Business Park, Spain
Office buildings for the San Sebastian de Los Reyes Business Park, Spain

1992-93

The Goshikidai Marine Resort Complex, Kagawa-ken, Japan (*)
Housing, Corso Garibaldi, Milan, Italy

Ongoing works

Extension to the Portello Sud area at the Milan Trade Fair, Milan, Italy (*)
New branch for the Schmidtbank and redevelopment of the

surrounding area with the creation of a new square,
Limbach-Oberfrohna, Germany (*)

Competitions

1969

New Hospital, Piacenza, Italy
with architects Carozzi and Rozzi; joint winning entry

1981

Park with two schools, Lago d'Iseo (Brescia), Italy

1983

Master Plan for the Parc de la Villette, international competition, Paris, France

1986

New National Theatre, international competition, Tokyo, Japan (*)

1988

Ryoma Sakamoto Memorial Hall, international competition, Kochi City, Japan (*)

1989

New Offices for Bayer Italia and sister companies Agfa and Miles, competition by invitation, Milan, Italy (*)

1990

"Berlin Morgen: Ideen für das Herz einer Großstadt", invited Consultation, Berlin, Germany (*)

1991

San Donato Milanese Town Center, invited consultation, San Donato Milanese (Milan), Italy (*)
Business Center in the Garibaldi-Repubblica Area, competition by invitation, Milan, Italy (*)
with Marco Romano

1992

New UNICEM Offices,

competition by invitation, San Mauro Torinese (Turin), Italy

1993

Master Plan for the redevelopment of an area in the Spree-Insel quarter of Berlin, international competition, Berlin, Germany

1994

Rathdown Civic Office, international competition, Dunlaoghaire (Dublin), Eire
Fifty Churches for the year 2000, competition for a new parish center in the Acilia area, Rome, Italy
Residential Quarter, competition by invitation, Urayasu New Town Tokyo Bay, Japan
Al Ahlia Commercial Center, competition by invitation, Dubai, United Arab Emirates
Yokohama International Port Terminal, international competition, Yokohama, Japan (*)
Competition by invitation for a new church at Desio, (Milan), Italy

1995

New Taichung Town Center, international competition, Taiwan, ROC
The Center is elsewhere. Suburbs and new centrality in the metropolitan area, invited consultation, Triennale di Milano, Italy

Writings by Mario Bellini
1960-95

The writings marked with an asterisk are also cited in the selected bibliographies for the technical descriptions of the projects and works

1960
"I baroni rampanti del movimento moderno. Tre generazioni nel dopoguerra italiano" (with R. Orefice and L. Zanon Dal Bo), *Superfici*, special issue, May 1960, pp. 23-30; see also no. 1, March 1961, pp. 7-9.
1961
"Cavalieri, libertini e Frères Maçon sulla scena milanese", *Superfici*, no. 1, March, pp. 39-40.
1964
"Sei domande a otto designers – M.Bellini", *Edilizia Moderna*, no. 85, pp. 8-11.
1966
"Superfici a tensione costante", *Linea Struttura*, no. 1, pp. 72-73.
"Campo di intervento del design nell'ufficio moderno", *Design Italia*, no. 3-4, September-December, pp. 115-118.
1968
"Notizie e novità di design", *Ottagono*, no. 9, April, p. 106.
"Chiara lampada per la Flos", *Ottagono*, no. 11, October, pp. 88-89.
L'architettura dell'interno (edited by Società Cassina SpA), published to mark the opening of the Cassina Showroom in Via Durini, 11 December 1968, Milan.
1969
"La casa di un designer", *Ottagono*, no. 12, January, pp. 24-35.
1970
"Un solo ambiente, tanti spazi circolari", *Domus*, no. 487, June, pp. 18-21.
"I sedili" (notes for a language of home-living edited by M. Bellini and M. Romano), pp. 86-93.

"Un'esperienza di design", *Ottagono*, no. 19, December, pp. 48-49.
1971
"Mario Bellini per la Olivetti", *Domus*, no. 494, January, pp. 32-41.
1972
"Ristorante 'Tondorante' a Bard", in G. Aloi, *Ristoranti*, Hoepli, Milan, pp. 137-142.
1973
"Automobile Kar-a-Sutra", *Bolaffi Arte*, June, pp. 75-77.
"Divisumma 18 Divisumma 28 Logos 68", *Domus*, no. 529, December, pp. 36-39.
1973-74
"In principio erat Logos", *In*, no. 12, December-January, p. 74.
"Le tentazioni", extract from *In*, no. 12, December-January.
1974
"Sequenza-Kit: 'Il design italiano'. Audiovisivo di Mario Bellini", *Environmedia*, no. 1, pp. 26-27.
1977
"Il design e le sue prospettive disciplinari", proceedings from the conference at accompanying the exhibition: "Il design italiano negli anni '50", organized by Centro Kappa under the patronage of the Lombardy Region, pp. 56-58.
"Per ufficio", *Domus*, no. 566, January, pp. 41-43.
1978
"Dallo studio di S. Gerolamo al Pianeta Ufficio" (with G. Origlia), *Sumo*, no. 1, January-February, pp. 2-8 (part one); *Sumo*, no. 2, March-April, pp. 9-13 (part two).
"Mario Bellini designer" (edited Società Cassina spa), published for the Cologne Furniture Fair,

17-22 January 1978.
1979
"Ma che cos'è questo design", *Casa Vogue*, no. 93, April.
"Disegnare una sedia", *Corriere della Sera*, 22 September.
"Questa casa è soltanto la mia casa", *Gran Bazaar*, November-December, pp. 106-107.
1980
"L'architetto e l'automobile", *Abitare*, no. 187, September, pp. 82-89.
"Un album tutto da mangiare", *Corriere della Sera*, 20 September.
1981
"Editorial", *Album. Progetto mangiare* (yearbook of projects and material culture edited by Mario Bellini), no. 1, Electa, Milan.
"Il proprio e l'improprio", *Gran Bazaar*, September-October, pp. 162-163.
"Presenza e assenza", *Gran Bazaar*, September-October, p. 187.
1982
"A Tokyo", *Ottagono*, no. 64, March, pp. 82-85.
"Gli uffici open space sono spiagge affollate", *Ufficio Stile*, no. 4, pp. 23-26.
"Showroom 'Interdecor' a Tokyo", *Domus*, no. 628, May, pp. 77-79.
"Victoria", *Ottagono*, no. 67, September, pp. 76-77.
"Sempre più brutte", *Le grandi automobili*, no. 1, Autumn, pp. 96-97.
1983
"Intervento sull'arredo urbano", monograph published by the Azienda Energetica Municipale di Milan.
"Un possibile futuro" (edited by

Società Artemide SpA), published following a round table organized for the Salone del Mobile, Milan.
"Dessiner le bureau", *L'Empire du bureau*, exhibition catalogue.
"Editorial", *Album. Progetto Ufficio* (yearbook of projects and material culture edited by Mario Bellini), no. 2, Electa, Milan.
"Humaniser le bureau de demain", in C. Davidson, M. Gagné et al., *Le bureau de demain – Actes du deuxième colloque sur la qualité de vie au travail*, Université de Montréal, Faculté de l'Aménagement, pp. 13-24.
"Il designer e l'industria", *Per chi lavora il designer*, proceedings from a conference organzied by the CGIL-Camera del lavoro territoriale di Milano, Ediesse, Rome, pp. 21-26.

1984
"Ich zeichne weiter", *Umriss*, no. 1-2, p. 9.
"Work & Environment", *Omni*, April, pp. 118-121.
Il cuoio: storia, tecnologia, design, (edited by Studio Prospettiva), catalogue for an exhibition held at Potenza, 9-19 May, Università della Basilicata, Mazzotta, pp. 99-105.
"L'architettura, gli arredi, le macchine...", *Design & Industria*, no. 2, July, p. 3.
"Falso problema", *Modo*, no. 71-72, August-September, p. 71.
Arredo urbano oggi, catalogue published by the Comune di Faenza, September-November.
"Storia di macchine e di sedie", *Modo*, no. 73, October, p. 56.
"Arredamento e città", *Modo*, no.

74, November, p. 57.
"Parole, culture, contesti", *Modo*, no. 75, December, p. 52.

1985
"Lo stile assente", *Modo*, no. 76, January-February.
"Lo stile presente", *Modo*, no. 77, March, p. 35.
"I mattoni di Louis Kahn", *Modo*, no. 78, April, p. 43.
"La fine di un ciclo", *Modo*, no. 79, May, p. 37.
"La 'carta' da calcolo", *Modo*, no. 80, June, p. 29.

1986
"Introduzione", pp. 13-17 (vol. *Saggi*); "Pensate architetti alla casa degli uomini" (with G. Teyssot), pp. 9-13 (vol. *Progetti*), in G. Teyssot (ed.), *Il Progetto Domestico – la casa dell'uomo archetipi e prototipi*, exhibition catalogue, 2 vols., Electa – XVII Triennale di Milano, Milan.
"Anche le parole sono materiale da costruzione", *Domus*, no. 670, March.
"Il Progetto Domestico", *Domus*, no. 671, April.
"Fiera e città", *Domus*, no. 672, May.
"Arredo urbano, falso problema", *Domus*, no. 673, June.
"Un nodo cruciale", *Domus*, no. 674, July-August.
"Architettura e design: considerazioni", *Domus*, no. 675, September.
"Abitare la macchina", *Domus*, no. 676, October.
"Automobili e immobili", *Domus*, no. 677, November.
"Esposizioni e progetto", *Domus*, no. 678, December.

1987
"La carrozzeria dell'architettura",

Domus, no. 679, January.
"Traffico urbano e forma urbis", *Domus*, no. 680, February.
"Progetto, disegno, segno, indizio", *Domus*, no. 681, March.
"La durata del progetto", *Domus*, no. 682, April.
"Le sedie degli architetti", *Domus*, no. 683, May.
"Il progetto celibe", *Domus*, no. 684, June.
"Le facciate", *Domus*, no. 685, July-August.
"Il design come spettacolo", *Domus*, no. 686, September.
"Le Corbusier ancora da scoprire", *Domus*, no. 687, October.
"Potere dell'architettura", *Domus*, no. 688, November.
"Tabù", *Domus*, no. 689, December.

1988
"Tecnica e creatività", *Domus*, no. 690, January.
"Di chi è la città", *Domus*, no. 691, February.
"Horror vacui", *Domus*, no. 692, March.
"Opere pubbliche e interesse privato", *Domus*, no. 693, April.
"L'insegnamento del Giappone", *Domus*, no. 694, May.
"No comment", *Domus*, no. 695, June.
"Il verde riparatore", *Domus*, no. 696, July-August.
"Disegno industriale e Disegno di mobili", *Domus*, no. 697, September.
"Le città del mondo e il futuro delle metropoli", *Domus*, no. 698, October.
"Che fare dell'edilizia?", *Domus*, no. 699, November.
"Una tecnica sovversiva", *Domus*, no. 700, December.

1989
Milano – Architetture per la città 1980-1990, foreword by Mario Bellini, Editoriale Domus, Milan, pp. 6-7.
"Dal design per l'industria all'industria del 'design'", *Domus*, no. 701, January.
"Una falsa democrazia che uccide le città", *Domus*, no. 702, February.
"I gioielli degli architetti", *Domus*, no. 703, March.
"C.A.D.", *Domus*, no. 704, April.
"L'ultima avanguardia", *Domus*, no. 705, May.
"Moderno & Contemporaneo", *Domus*, no. 706, June.
"La tecnica è nuda", *Domus*, no. 707, July-August.
"Wovon man nicht sprechen kann, darüber muss man schweigen"", *Domus*, no. 708, September.
"Prototipo & Tipo – La fatica di Sisifo", *Domus*, no. 709, October.
"Firmato", *Domus*, no. 710, November.
"Cosa si fa a Milano?", *Domus*, no. 711, December.

1990
"Costruire come arte e l'arte del costruire", *Domus*, no. 712, January.
"Elogio del pluralismo", *Domus*, no. 714, March.
"Neoisterismo milanese", *Domus*, no. 715, April.
"Grado zero", *Domus*, no. 716, May.
"Ultimo appello", *Domus*, no. 717, June.
"Il paese delle meraviglie", *Domus*, no. 718, July-August.
"Il grande numero", *Domus*, no. 719, September.

"Ancora sul progetto", *Domus*, no. 720, October.
"Carta bianca", *Domus*, no. 721, November.
"Architectures publiques", *Domus*, no. 722, December.
1991
"Berlin domani", *Domus*, no. 723, January.
Mario Bellini (ed.), *The International Design Yearbook 6*, Abbeville Press-Publishers, New York.
Berlin Morgen: Ideen für das Herz einer Großstadt, ed. V.M. Lampugnani and M. Mönninger (exhibition catalogue), Deutsches Architektur Museum, Frankfurt and Hatje Verlag, Stuttgart, pp. 88-93.
"Manutenzione", *Domus*, no. 724, February.
"Guardare le fotografie", *Domus*, no. 725, March.
"Firmato: 'Anonimo'", *Domus*, no. 726, April.
"La mia città preferita", *Town and Design*, April.
"L'architettura della città e la città dell'architettura", *Domus*, no. 727, May.
"Questioni di stile", *Domus*, no. 728, June.
"La conservazione che distrugge", *Domus*, no. 729, July-August.
"Mostrare l'architettura", *Domus*, no. 730, September.
"Oltre l'architettura", *Domus*, no. 731, October.
"Il virus astratto", *Domus*, no. 732, November.
"Le parole saranno ancora materiale da costruzione", *Domus*, no. 733, December.
"Mario Bellini. Revitalising a multiple heart", *Architectural Design*, monographic issue. (*)
"Berlin tomorrow. International Architectural Visions", no. 92, published as a part of *Architectural Design*, pp. 20-29.
1992
"Architecture and cities", *JA* (Japan Architect), no. 3, July, pp. 172-179.
"Lo stile del nostro tempo", *Abitare*, August.
1993
"Risonare-Vivre Club; Tokyo Design Center", *GA Japan*, no. 3, pp. 104-107, 150-157.
"Pareri autorevoli sul Nuovo Corso di Laurea in Disegno Industriale", *Sinopie*, no. 7, April, pp. 9-10.
1994
"Tokyo Design Center", *Axis*, vol. 50, 1 January.
1994 Obayashi Calendar, has writings by Mario Bellini on a number of his projects, Obayashi Corporation, Tokyo.
"Extra Dry", *Abitare*, no. 333, October 1994, pp. 212-213.
"Un allestimento di luce per le architetture del Rinascimento", *Exporre*, no. 20, June (*).
Bauwelt, no. 20, 20 May.
1995
"Ci salveranno le vecchie caffettiere?", *Domus*, no. 767, January, pp. 78-79.
"Idee di case", *Domus*, October, pp. 55-57 (edited text of a conversation between Vittorio Magnago Lampugnani and Mario Bellini in July 1995).

Editorials as editor-in-chief of the monthly review "Domus" 1986-1991

1986

no. 670, March, *Anche le parole sono materiale da costruzione*
no. 671, April, *Il Progetto Domestico*
no. 672, May, *Fiera e città*
no. 673, June, *Arredo urbano, falso problema*
no. 674, July-August, *Un nodo cruciale*
no. 676, October, *Abitare la macchina*
no. 677, November, *Automobili e immobili*
no. 678, December,*Esposizioni e progetto*

1987

no. 679, January, *La carrozzerie dell'architettura*
no. 680, February, *Traffico urbano e forma urbis*
no. 681, March, *Progetto, disegno, segno, indizio*
no. 682, April, *La durata del progetto*
no. 683, May, *Le sedie degli architects*
no. 684, June, *Il progetto celibe*
no. 685, July-August, *Le facciate*
no. 686, September, *I design come spettacolo*
no. 687, October, *Le Corbusier ancora da scoprire*
no. 688, November, *Potere dell'architettura*
no. 689, December, *Tabù*

1988

no. 690, January, *Tecnica e creatività*
no. 691, February, *Di chi è la città*
no. 692, March, *Horror vacui*
no. 693, April, *Opere pubbliche e interesse privato*
no. 694, May, *L'insegnamento del Giappone*
no. 695, June, *No comment*

no. 696, July-August, *Il verde riparatore*
no. 697, September, *Disegno industriale e Disegno di mobili*
no. 698, October, *Le città del mondo e il futuro delle metropoli*
no. 699, November, *Che fare dell'edilizia?*
no. 700, December, *Una tecnica sovversiva*

1989

no. 701, Jabuary, *Dal design per l'industria*
no. 702, February, *Una falsa democrazia che uccide le città*
no. 703, March, *I gioielli degli architects*
no. 704, April, *C.A.D.*
no. 705, May, *L'ultima avanguardia*
no. 706, June, *Moderno & Contemporaneo*
no. 707, July-August, *La tecnica è nuda*
no. 708, September, *Wovon man nicht sprechen kann, darüber muss man schweigen"*
no. 709, October, *Prototipo & Tipo – La fatica di Sisifo*
no. 710, November, *Firmato – Signed*
no. 711, December, *Cosa si fa a Milano?*

1990

no. 712, January, *Costruire come arte e l'arte del costruire*
no. 714, March, *Elogio del pluralismo*
no. 715, April, *Neoisterismo milanese*
no. 716, May, *Grado zero*
no. 717, June, *Ultimo appello*
no. 718, July-August, *Il paese delle meraviglie*
no. 719, September, *Il grande numero*

no. 720, October, *Ancora sul progetto*
no. 721, November, *Carta bianca*
no. 722, December, *Architectures publiques*

1991

no. 723, January, *Berlin domani*
no. 724, February, *Manutenzione*
no. 725, March, *Guardare le fotografie*
no. 726, April, *Firmato: 'anonimo'*
no. 727, May, *L'architettura della città e la città dell'architettura*
no. 728, June, *Questioni di stile*
no. 729, July-August, *La conservazione che distrugge*
no. 730, September, *Mostrare l'architettura*
no. 731, October, *Oltre l'architettura*
no. 732, November, *Il virus astratto*
no. 733, December, *Le parole saranno ancora materiale da costruzione*

Bibliography

The writings marked with an asterisk are also cited in the selected bibliographies for the technical descriptions of the projects and works

1967
"Mario Bellini: mobili e poltrone di un industrial designer", *Ottagono*, no. 5, April, pp. 38-49.
"Nuovi disegni di Mario Bellini", *Domus*, no. 452, July, pp. 46-50.
L'arte moderna, vol. XIV, no. 119, F.lli Fabbri, Milan.
1969
G. P., "Successo a Milano", *Domus*, no. 471, February, pp. 22-29.
1971
D. Rowlands, "Object and image maker", *Design*, no. 267, March.
P. C. Santini and S. Yanagi in collaboration with S. A. Matsutake, "Designs by Mario Bellini – Poetry in form", *Japan Interior design*, no. 153, December, pp. 17-54.
1972
The new domestic landscape, exhibition catalogue, The Museum of Modern Art, New York.
P. Fossati, *Il design in Italia 1945-1972*, Einaudi, Turin.
1973
"Le tentazioni", *Ottagono*, no. 31, December, pp. 76-79.
I. Sannazzaro, "Il prodotto dell' arredamento alla XV Triennale di Milano", *L' Industria del Mobile*, December, pp. 506-513.
1974
"Vi spieghiamo cos'è un designer", interview, *Quattrosoldi*, March, p. 71.
E. Frateili, "Design e attualità figurative", *Qui arte contemporanea*, May, pp. 52-57.
"Dialogue with designers", interview, *Interior Design*, July, p. 60.

1975
"Pianeta ufficio", *Domus*, no. 546, May, pp. 36-37.
1977
"Tavoli", *Ottagono*, a. 12, no. 46, September, pp. 70-73.
1978
"Mario Bellini – Creator of humanistic forms", *Japan Interior Design*, no. 232, July, pp. 21-64.
M. Lavrillier, *50 Designers dal 1950 al 1975*, Görlich, Novara, pp. 108-119.
1979
Progettare con l'oro (edited by P. C. Santini), exhibition catalogue, Palazzo Strozzi, Firenze, Nuova Vallecchi, Firenze.
1980
G. Ballo, "A Palazzo Strozzi: progettare con l'oro", *Ottagono*, a. 15, no. 56, March, pp. 102-105.
A. Grassi and A. Pansera, *Atlante del design italiano 1940-1980*, Fabbri, Milan.
I. Vercelloni, *1970-1980 Dal Design al post design*, Condé Nast, Milan.
"Così la pensa...", interview, *Sumo*, no. 2, March-April.
"Wer macht design", interview, *Das Haus*, September.
1981
"La vita è segno", interview, *Gap Casa*, no. 15, January-February, pp. 17-21.
D. Puppa, "Tesori antinflazione sulla tavola", *Modo*, no. 37, March, pp. 30-31.
1982
V. Gregotti, *Il disegno nel prodotto industriale – Italia 1860-1980*, Electa, Milan.
"Colloqui di Modo: Non finirò designer", interview, *Modo*, no. 53, October, pp. 24-27.

1983
Design Process – Olivetti 1908-1983, Comunità, Milan.
E. Frateili, *Il disegno industriale italiano 1928-1981*, Celid, Turin.
"Le interviste di AD – Mario Bellini", interview, *AD*, no. 20, January, pp. 12, 14, 16.
D. Polaczek, "Mario Bellini", *Frankfurter Allgemeine Magazin*, Heft 172, June, pp. 12-19, 33.
N. Pallini, "Come è difficile inventare una sedia", interview, *Il Secolo XIX*, 2 November.
1984
H. J. Weimann, "Design-Warum ein guter Tisch einer Skulptur gleicht", *Ambiente Wohnen International*, February, pp. 120-134.
"Design Focus – Mario Bellini", *The Bystander*, vol. 1, no. 2, February-March.
B. Brennan, "Bravo Bellini – Living Interview", *Vogue Living*, April, pp. 22-23.
C. Wood, "Mario Bellini – Interview", *Design World*, no. 4, pp. 30-35.
"Il linguaggio della tecnica, le tecnologie del linguaggio", *Design & Industria*, no. 2, July, pp. 4-5.
"Why Italian industrial design is sweeping the world", *International Business Week*, 3 September, pp. 34-37.
G. Carrari, "Così i vip del design reinventano la città – Dieci proposte per la nuova Milano", *La Repubblica*, 29 November.
P. Mc Guire, "Mario Bellini", *The Architectural Review*, no. 1053, November.
"Una centrale nel verde", *Aem notizie*, no. 4, November.

1985
O. Pivetta, "Costruire il domani –
Tsukuba: L' Italia in vetrina",
Costruire, no. 27, March,
pp. 138-141.
G. Volpi, "Cerca turismo il naviglio
di Paderno, mezzo miliardo
cancellerà l'abbandono",
Il Giornale, 22 April.
P. Arosio, "Parte da Baggio la
riscossa delle periferie storiche",
L'Unità, 26 April.
M. Pria, "Proposte per la nuova
Milano", *Mondo Economico*, 24
June.
"La Bellezza – Braccio di ferro
Mario Bellini-Michele De Lucchi",
interview, *Modo*, no. 81,
July-August, pp. 14-19.
E. Besussi, "Tasti e visori e nel
mezzo un Luigi XVI", *La
Repubblica*, 24 September.
"Mario Bellini", *Axis*, vol. 14,
Winter.
R. De Fusco, *Storia del design*,
Laterza, Bari.
G. Gramigna, *1950-1980
Repertorio*, Mondadori, Milan.
1986
AA.VV., *Un'industria per il design*,
Lybra Immagine, Milan.
N. Aspesi, "Arriva Ines robot
ribelle", *La Repubblica*, 16
January. (*)
S. Dal Pozzo, "Qui telecomando
io", *Panorama*, 20 January,
pp. 120-123.
A. Pozzi, "Triennale, l'uomo
domestico tra capanne e case
mobili", *L'Unità*, 18 January.
F. Doveil, "Tutti a casa", *Modo*, no.
86, January-February, pp. 24-29.
C. Morozzi, "Il progetto
domestico: la casa dell'uomo",
La mia casa, no. 184,
January-February.

V. Gregotti, "Lungo Viaggio
attraverso la casa", *Panorama*,
16 February, p. 19. (*)
K. Singleton, "Bricks and words
at Milan Triennale", *International
Herald Tribune*, 8-9 February. (*)
"La casa come l'abito è un mezzo
per comunicare", interview,
La mia casa, no. 184,
January-February. (*)
"La questione dell'abitazione"
(edited by S.Milesi), round table
during the exhibition "Il Progetto
Domestico alla XVII Triennale di
Milano", *Casabella*, no. 522,
March. (*)
A. Grassi, A. Pansera, *L'Italia del
design*, Marietti, Casale
Monferrato.
Italia disegno 1946-1986 (edited
by R. Littman, R. Zorzi, G. Dorfles,
V. Gregotti, L. Ponti), exhibition
catalogue – Museo Rufino
Tamayo, Mexico City.
V. Magnago Lampugnani, "Design
– Form und Farbe für den Alltag",
Merian Mailand (monographic
issue on Milan), 10-38, pp. 56-57.
A. Dell' Acqua Bellavitis, "Mario
Bellini – Al centro del design, l'
uomo", *Costruire per abitare*,
no. 38, March, pp. 169-170.
G. Carrari, "Con me ritornerà la
grande Domus", interview,
Corriere della Sera, 19 March.
"XVII Triennale di Milano – Il
progetto domestico", *Domus*,
no. 671, April, pp. 44-73. (*)
J. Burney, *Renaissance Man*,
3, 16 May.
"Ergonomie als Vorwand",
interview, *Wirtschafts*, no. 29, July,
pp. 91, 93.
A. Mangeri, "Il Progetto
domestico e i luoghi del lavoro",
Contract, November, pp. 18-20.

*Entries in the Architecture
Competition for the New National
Theater, Tokyo, Japan*, Japan
Association for Construction
Government Buildings, p. 171. (*)
1987
B. Radice, *Gioielli di architetti*,
Electa, Milan, pp. 9-13.
C. McCarty, *Mario Bellini:
designer,* exhibition catalogue,
The Museum of Modern Art,
New York. (*)
*I segni dell'habitat. Tecnologie e
design d'Italia*, catalogue of
exhibition promoted by ICE, pp.
16-17, Electa, Milan.
"Mario Bellini: design, tecnologia
e ricerca – L'artigiano del 2000",
interview, *Casa oggi*, no. 151-152,
January-February, pp. 22-27.
M. Romanelli, "Mario Bellini-Sedie
per ufficio Vitra", *Domus*, no. 680,
February, pp. 38-51.
"Bellini" (by A. Hanna, C. McCarty,
C. Pearlman), *Industrial Design*,
May-June. (*)
C. Kent, "Italian Style", interview,
Inland Architect, May-June,
pp. 64-65.
S. Slesin, "27 years of Mario
Bellini's deft designs", and
P. Leigh Brown, "Umanizing
electronics and technology",
The New York Times (home
section), 25 June. (*)
M. Sorkin, "Mario Bellini",
The village voice, 21 June.
T. Forsman, "Mind over machine –
the Bellini touch", *The Record*, 26
June.
M. Albertazzi, "Versatilità e
inventiva del designer Mario
Bellini", *Il Progresso*, 24 June.
C. De Seta, "Dolci tecnologie di
Bellini", *Corriere della Sera*, 27
June. (*)

F. Colombo, "Bellini e lo scrigno
per tesori", *La Stampa*, 7 July.
S. Trincia, "Com'è sensuale quel
computer", *Il Messaggero*, 24 July.
R. Zorzi, "Vorticosa corsa al
nuovo", *Il Sole 24 Ore*,
23 August. (*)
J. Russell, "Sensuous Designs
by Mario Bellini in Museum
Show", *The New York Times*,
28 August. (*)
T. Hine, "Poetry in everyday
objects: the designs of Mario
Bellini", *Philadelphia Inquirer*,
23 August. (*)
1988
G. Bosoni, F. G. Confalonieri,
*Paesaggio del design italiano
1972-1988*, Edizioni di Comunità,
Milan.
Mario Bellini. Architetture, edited
by E.Ranzani, catalogue-book,
Electa, Milan. (*)
P. C. Santini, "Elogio di Mario
Bellini", *Ottagono*, no. 88, March.
"Macchine, mobili e architetture",
interview by B. Gravagnuolo, *N.C.
Design*, no. 3, July, pp. 14-18.
"La torre di salita", *Casa Vogue*,
no. 200, September.
A. Ubertazzi, "Incontro con un
protagonista. Il design di Mario
Bellini", interview, *Office
Furniture*, 1988-89, pp. 2-33; also
in *Habitat Ufficio*, supplement to
no. 31.
Milano Progetti Ottantanove,
Comune di Milan. (*)
1989
*Milano. Architetture per la città,
1980-1990*, Editoriale Domus,
Rozzano (Milan), pp. 62, 116-119,
130. (*)
M. Romanelli, "Le forme di Mario
Bellini", *L'etichetta*, no. 23, Spring.
"'Italian Art in the 20th Century', a

Londra", *Domus*, no. 704, April.
P. A. C., "Il pannello intelligente", *Casabella*, no. 557, May,
pp. 36-39. (*)
"Centro Esposizioni e Congressi di Villa Erba", *Frames*, no. 4,
July-September, pp. 36-41. (*)
"Le stanze dell'arte", *Abitare*,
September.
L'Architecture demain…,
published for the Deuxième
Salon International de
l'Architecture, 28 October-5
November, Parigi, BL Associés sa
– Techniques & Architecture, Paris.
"Showroom Cassina Japan",
Nikkei Architecture, no. 11,
pp.248-252. (*)
"Showroom Cassina Japan",
Shotenkenchiku, no. 12, vol. 34,
December, pp. 194-195. (*)

1990
"Showroom Cassina Japan", *Icon*,
no. 1, vol. 21, pp. 88-92. (*)
"Centro Esposizioni e Congressi
di Villa Erba e ampliamento Fiera
di Milano", *Exporre*, no. 3, March,
pp. 8, 12. (*)
"Ich hasse die Design Welt",
Manager Magazine, May, pp.
332-339.
"Yokohama Business Park, *Nikkei
Architecture*, no. 5, pp. 90-96. (*)
Yokohama Business Park,
Shinkenchiku, no. 6, pp. 289-295.
(*)
"Centro Esposizioni e Congressi
di Villa Erba", *Vetro-Spazio*, no. 18,
September, pp. 10-16. (*)
"Centro esposizioni e congressi di
Villa Erba"
L'Arca, no. 44, December, p. 106.
(*)
F. Moschini, "Mario Bellini. Uffici
Centrale Aem, Cassano d'
Adda-Milano", *Domus*, no. 722,

December, pp. 38-47. (*)
1991
"Yokohama Business Park",
Shinkenchiku, no. 1, pp. 360-363. (*)
"Yokohama Business Park",
Shoten Kenchiku, no. 1, vol. 36,
January, pp. 174-179. (*)
"Centro Esposizioni e Congressi
di Villa Erba", *Europronto*, no. 1,
vol. 1, pp. 21-27. (*)
"Berlin Morgen", *Frankfurter
Allgemeine Zeitung* no. 4,
January. (*)
Nikkei Architecture, interview, no.
2, pp. 44-49.
Design Journal, no. 55,
January-February, pp. 66-67.
"Yokohama Business Park" *Nikkei
Architecture*, no. 2, pp. 189-191. (*)
"Centro Esposizioni e Congressi
di Villa Erba", *Costruzioni
metalliche*, no. 2, pp. 65-73. (*)
"Concorso 'Berlin Morgen'",
Domus, no. 725, March,
pp. 54-63. (*)
"Yokohama Business Park", *Japan
Landscape*, no. 19, pp. 78-83. (*)
"Mario Bellini – Progetto per la
Fiera di Milano al Portello Sud"
(report by E.Ranzani), *Domus*, no.
728, June, pp. 25-41. (*)
F. Purini, "Fiera di Milano – Sul
progetto Bellini", *Domus*, no. 728,
June, pp. 42-43. (*)
"Centro Esposizioni e Congressi
di Villa Erba" *A x A*, no. 2,
September, pp. 4-11. (*)
"Yokohama Business Park",
Kenchiku Gaho, no. 226, vol. 27,
November, pp. 77-85. (*)
R. Sanders, "Der Designer hat
abgedankt!", *Der Feinschmecker*,
no. 11, November, pp. 158-160.
"Showroom Cassina Japan",
Interior Design, December,
pp. 86-89. (*)

1992
G. Bosoni, "Big Adventure in
Italy", *Gulliver*, no. 46, pp.
132-143.
"Centro civico di San Donato
Milanese", *Quinto Miglio*, no. 4,
April. (*)
"Tokyo Design Center", *Nikkei
Architecture*, no. 4,
pp. 164-169. (*)
"Centro civico di San Donato
Milanese", *Il Cittadino*, no. 5,
May. (*)
Centro città San Donato Milanese,
catalogue, Comune di San Donato
Milanese. (*)
"Mario Bellini – Exhibition and
Congress Center", *A+U*, no. 260,
May, pp. 86-95. (*)
"Tokyo Design Center",
Shinkenchiku , no. 5,
pp. 223-234. (*)
"Tokyo Design Center", *Shoten
Kenchiku*, no. 5, vol. 37, May,
pp. 170-179. (*)
"Tokyo Design Center", *FP*,
no. 49, pp. 61-65. (*)
E. Morteo, "Mario Bellini –
Personal Computer Olivetti
Quaderno", *Domus*, no. 741,
September, pp. 79-83.
"Risonare-Vivre Club Complex",
Nikkei Architecture, no. 8,
pp. 112-125. (*)
"Risonare-Vivre Club Complex",
Shinkenchiku, no. 9, pp. 235-248. (*)
"Risonare-Vivre Club Complex",
Shoten Kenchiku, no. 9,
September, pp. 170-181. (*)
Seven Seas, no. 50, September,
pp. 28-31.
AT (Architecture Magazine),
no. 10, October, pp. 5-34.
Brutus, interview, 10-1,
pp. 134-135.
F. Maki, "Mario Bellini – The Tokyo

Design Center", *Domus*, no. 743,
November, pp. 36-43. (*)
R. Sanders, "Personality – Ein
Mann, der sich in Frage stellt",
Intercity, no. 12, pp. 26-28.
*Progetti per Milano – Concorso di
Idee per il polo
direzionale-finanziario nell'area
Garibaldi-Repubblica*, catalogue,
Abitare Segesta Cataloghi,
Milan. (*)
"Centro Esposizioni e Congressi
di Villa Erba", *L'Architettura della
tecnologia*, E.A. Fiera di Bologna,
pp. 35-53. (*)
"Yokohama Business Park", *YBP
Works*, Nomura Real Estate. (*)
1993
E. Morteo, M. Romanelli, "Gli
arredi degli architetti – Mario
Bellini", interview, *Domus*, no.
748, April, pp. 72-73, 76-79.
Blueprint Extra, monographic
issue on the Villa Erba
International Exhibition and
Conference Center. (*)
E. Morteo, "La serra dei
congressi", *Abitare*, no. 321,
September, pp. 186-193. (*)
E. Ranzani, "Mario Bellini –
Stazione di Ristoro per reti
autostradali", *Domus*, no. 755,
December, pp. 36-41. (*)
1994
"Mario Bellini, architetto e
designer", *OFX Office
International*, no. 16,
January-February.
"Progettando con Mario Bellini",
interview di R. U. Lepreri, *Domina*,
no. 58, February.
"The Renaissance from
Brunelleschi to Michelangelo",
article by C. Assey, *Financial
Times*, 16-17 April. (*)
"La luce del Rinascimento",

Abitare, no. 330, June,
pp. 182-189. (*)
C. De Seta, "I modelli della città
ideale", *Corriere della Sera*, 5
November. (*)
1995
"La poetica del luogo, il confronto
con la Storia", interview by L.
Servadio, *Casa Oggi*, no. 248,
April, pp. 24-29.
"Costruire attorno a una
magnolia", *Casa Oggi*, no. 248,
April, pp. 30-31 (Two Residential
Buildings in Via Madonnina). (*)
"Una nuova Fiera a Milano",
Ufficio Stile, no. 3, May-June, pp.
54-61. (*)
C. Gardner, "Italy's urban space
man", *World Architecture*, no. 39,
pp. 112-115.
*Il centro altrove – Periferie e
nuove centralità nelle aree
metropolitane*, exhibition
catalogue, Electa – Triennale di
Milano, Milan 1995, pp. 221,
236-238.
"Re-Officing Mario Bellini
Associati", *Eciffo*, vol. 27,
Autumn, pp. 10-26. (*)
"Proyectar para la ciudad",
La Prensa, 10 January, pp. 8-9.
"Mario Bellini, un notable teòrico
pràtico", *La Nacion*, 11 January,
pp. 1-3.
M. Videla, "La arquitectura,
combinaciòn milagrosa entre
tecnica, tradiciòn y naturaleza",
El Cronista, 25 January, pp. 4-5.
J. Glusberg, "Mario Bellini: la rica
dimensiòn del spacio",
El Cronista, 11 October,
pp. 2-3, 12.
"Tradición, tecnologia y
naturaleza", *La Prensa*, 7 February,
pp. 6-7.

**Studio Mario Bellini
Associati Collaborators
from 1985 to 1995**

Massimo Adriante
Rina Agostino
Philip Allen
M. Grazia Angiolini
Paola Azzolini
Federico Barbero
Marisa Barda
Chiara Bellini
Claudio Bellini
Dario Bellini
Elena Bellini
Francesco Bellini
Elena Beorchia
Rossella Bianchi
Giovanna Bonfanti
Edoardo Brambilla
Serio Brioschi
Elena Bruschi
Loretto Buti
Giovanni Cappelletti
Raffaele Cipolletta
Luca Clavarino
Christian Cornelius
Silvia Cortesi
Chiara Costa
Michael Costantin
Pierpaolo Curti
Olivia De Luca
Antonio Esposito
Sarah Felton
Edoardo Ferrari
Giuseppe Filiputti
Andrea Fiorentini
Frank Friedman
Massimo Giacon
Fabrizio Galli
Edoardo Germani
Stefano Grioni
Enza Gueli
Debra Haddock
Larry Lee
Pier Angelo Lissi
Alessandro Luvieri

Carlo Malnati
Carlo Mason
Masahiro Matsuno
Andrea Mazzullo
Gabi Mbaied
Hideo Miura
Luigi Morandi
Luigi Mura
Giorgio Origlia
Nicoletta Pallini
Doris Paridi
Marco Parravicini
Celestino Pedrazzini
Antonella Piazzoli
Terry Piazzoli
Marco Piccione
Pietro Pietromarchi
Giovanni Pigni
Vittorio Prina
Ermanno Ranzani
Vittorio Samarati
Marco Santagostino
Stefania Secondi
Katia Selle
Paola Seria
Donato Severo
David Sherriff
Romana Simeoni
Adriana Sinigaglia
Richard Sturgeon
Angelo Tirabosch
Agata Torricella
Davide Vianello
Lorenzo Viti
Claudia Viviani
Federica Wendler
Marco Zanibelli
Carlo Zocco
Angela Zuzzi

List of photographers

Gabriele Basilico, Milano
Mario Carrieri, Milano
Raffaele Cipolletta, Meda (Milano)
Fregoso/Basalto, La Spezia
Moreno Gentili, Como
Kawasumi Photograph Office,
Tokyo
Kuroda, Tokyo
Antonio Martinelli, Parigi
Norman Mc Grath, New York
Murai Inc., Fukui City
Nacasa & Partners Inc., Tokyo
Obayashi Corporation, Tokyo
Francesco Radino, Besozzo
(Varese)
Retoria V. Takase, Tokyo
Shinkenchiku-Sha Co. Ltd., Tokyo
Yoshio Shiratori, Tokyo
Shoten Kenchiku-Sha Publishing
Co. Ltd., Tokyo
Studio Crabb, Milano
Studio Gui, Milano

Printed in Italy
by Europrint, Treviso